Dandelions
and
Bad Hair Days

Untangling lives affected by depression and anxiety

An anthology of inspirational, original prose and poetry on the experience of mental illness compiled & edited by Suzie Grogan

Published in 2012 by Dotterel Press

ISBN: 978-0-9562869-8-7

Contents

Foreword by Marjorie Wallace CBE - Chief Executive, SANE

Dandelions and Bad Hair Days is a collection of moving confessionals from people with first-hand experience of mental illness and from carers who have witnessed their suffering. It offers a fascinating glimpse into the daily reality of living with such conditions as depression, anxiety, obsessive compulsive disorder and through times when they have felt suicidal.

Compiled from the blog posts of professional and amateur writers and fusing a colourful mix of poetry and prose, accounts range from the harrowing to the humorous. All contributors are united by a determination to fight their condition, despite difficult odds, and they share a depth of emotional sensitivity and self-awareness which is both admirable and humbling. I was particularly impressed by Nettie Edwards' exquisite descriptions of her emotional recovery and Nic Elgey's creative solution for helping herself and others.

This anthology is a testament to the therapeutic role of blogging for personal expression and its scope for harnessing a community of mutual supporters and followers.

From my own experience as a journalist, campaigner and founder and chief executive of the mental health charity SANE, I see combating the ignorance and stigma surrounding mental illness as one of the key challenges. It was one of the causes which inspired SANE's Black Dog campaign to raise awareness and address the growing challenge of depression and other mental illness, the Black Dog having been used from classical through to modern times as a universal metaphor for depression. Central to the campaign is the positioning of black dog sculptures in public spaces around the country, to act as a symbol to externalise moods and thoughts that are hard to communicate. We hope that through them, people will find a new language to express difficult inner feelings and seek help rather than suffer in isolation.

Perhaps the ultimate way to end discrimination is for the community of people affected by mental ill health to take the first few brave steps and tell their stories. The more we can build on their experiences, the more that understanding can be increased and attitudes altered. Suzie Grogan's anthology is to be commended for helping to build this momentum.

I urge anyone who wishes to read a self help book with a difference, or who wishes to learn about the human cost of mental illness, to read Dandelions and Bad Hair Day. I challenge them not to be inspired.

Introduction

Mental illness can affect anyone. No walk of life, career or privilege can offer you immunity. One in four people will experience mental ill health over their lifetime but there remains a stigma attached to the condition and discrimination is still common. Many have been unwilling to admit they need help, but although much remains to be done, as we entered the 21st century it became easier to raise the subject of mental health, partly due to the willingness of people in the public eye to stand up and admit they had sought treatment. In recent months, high profile deaths of sports stars and celebrities have once again brought the subject to the attention of a wider public. The emotional health and well-being of men in particular - frequently more reluctant to discuss their feelings openly - has been the focus of much discussion. Even the most 'macho' of sports men have been affected. No longer should we sing the refrain 'boys don't cry'....

As life appears to 'speed up', as new methods of communication become available and our ability to retreat from the world into peace and seclusion diminishes, so we find it harder to avoid the stresses of work, of family problems, of our finances. The world can crowd in on us from our desks as we surf the Internet; a tool capable of offering us wonderful opportunities to learn and communicate globally becomes an instrument capable of sweeping wave upon wave of stress over us. The world is opened to us but through a portal that has an equal capacity to isolate and intimidate. It can be hard to protect ourselves. I was one of the many who struggled.

In August 2010 I had been blogging for six weeks. My enthusiasm had not waned in the least, but I had started to ask myself 'why?' What was I seeking to achieve by writing 750 words at least three times a week and putting them out there?

Having been made redundant from my job as Development Manager for a local mental health charity and finding the local jobs market offered little that matched my physical abilities or mental capacity, I decided to return to freelance work. For 10 years I had been a researcher, largely into social exclusion and the labour market, writing analysis and strategy documents for the public and voluntary sectors. However, the economic downturn had restricted the money available for the kind of reports I wrote. I was under no illusion - many collected dust on the shelves of a local government office, unread. Striving as I had to be creative with the work I was commissioned to write; seeking new ways to present dry information to engage and enthuse, I had frequently found that my efforts were purely to preserve my own interest. A government strategy would last 12 months before something new was introduced and my work became obsolete. Did I really want to return to that, even had the money been there to support me?

I turned to a first love - writing. The blog was there to spur me on. It was a place to practice, to network with others in the 'blogosphere' and find inspiration. It quickly became clear as I engaged with other mums and dads in the parent blogging community that many wrote to feel less isolated. Very personal information was shared and subjects that came up time and again were depression and anxiety, even if they were not always the actual words employed to describe what the writer felt. As I sat to write another blog post it seemed safe to 'come out' to this crowd - hundreds of friendly people who were willing to support complete strangers through tough times. I wrote the first piece in this book. I was overwhelmed by the response I received and it encouraged me to think of my blog as a vehicle for other others to have their say - away from their own blog that may have dealt with a quite different subject matter. The No wriggling out of writing monthly mental health guest post was born.

This book is a tribute to all those people who were happy to share their experience via my blog. The pieces that follow vary widely - from a straightforward account of the experience of depression, to the heartbreak of a parent's loss of their child and the subject treated as an inspiration to creative writing. Poetry and prose combine to offer stories of suffering and pain, but also hope, laughter and life. Everyone involved in this book has experienced mental health issues, or has lived or worked with those who have. Authors are priests, writers, teachers and charity workers. Some find employment hard to find at the moment. They are mothers, fathers, sons, daughters and friends. They are everyone, all of us. This book could save your life.

Suzie Grogan 2012

Mental illness, motherhood and finding the real me

Suzie Grogan

So this is me - a freelance professional researcher and writer on topics as diverse as social exclusion, the poet John Keats, social and family history and women's' health issues. I have been published in many national and online magazines and blog at www.nowrigglingoutofwriting.wordpress.com.

I am also a wife and mother of two children who haven't yet realised how interesting their mother can be if given the chance. If you want to find out more about me see my website at www.suziegrogan.co.uk.

In 2006 I was diagnosed with and successfully treated for breast cancer (including reconstruction) and I have had Primary Lymphoedema since my teens. This has contributed to bouts of depression and health anxiety, prompting the establishment of the mental health page on my blog.

My name is Suzie and I have experienced mental illness. There I have said it. Not so difficult really, was it? Actually, it was difficult and for many people it is practically impossible to come out and express how mental or emotional distress has affected their lives. There is a real fear of the stigma attached to mental health issues and for me, as a wife and mother, professional woman and yes, a person in my own right, it is only now that I can truly sense how destructive any such perceived discrimination can be. For the past two years I have worked for the local mental health charity Mind in Taunton & West Somerset and have seen at first-hand how people struggle to re-engage with whatever passes for a normal life in the 21st century.

I can't remember when I experienced my first real bout of depression. I was an anxious child, and terrified teenager. I had a loving and secure childhood, with two younger siblings but with a father poorly with Parkinson's from his mid-40s onwards perhaps I took on some of his anxious nature. He was certainly incredibly superstitious and convinced the worst would always happen.

After I had my own children I was diagnosed with a form of Obsessive Compulsive Disorder (OCD). All parents are anxious but I took it to extremes, convinced that if I didn't follow certain rituals (such as making the beds properly, or laying the table with matching cutlery) some terrible accident would befall my family. I developed an eating disorder as a means of introducing some control into my life and was eventually desperate

3

enough to approach my GP. I was lucky to be offered Cognitive Behavioural Therapy (CBT) and the OCD became manageable, but the lingering thought that something I did, or failed to do, would bring some disaster on us all remained.

Unluckily for me this feeling seemed to be confirmed when, only in my early 40s, I was diagnosed with breast cancer in 2007. All my fears having come true, and despite coming through all the treatment successfully, I became swallowed up with anxiety about my health and I felt terrified of everything the future held for me. However now, at last, I feel there is light at the end of the tunnel, but (as I suspect many others who have experienced anxiety and depression would agree) even saying that phrase can fill you with dread at what you may bring down upon yourself. It is an on-going battle.

I have struggled with how my illness manifests itself in front of my children. It must be frightening to see your mother raging at herself for her inability to cope with the simplest setback. I have never thought it wrong to express your emotions in front of the family but there are limits and I must have exceeded them many times.

As a mother I knew I was supposed to bring up my son and daughter to be confident, caring people with a proper sense of who they were and what their place in the world might be. I was meant to give them all the opportunities I could to equip them for a future with choice and the ability to forge happy relationships with their peers. How was I supposed to do that when I had no sense of myself, no confidence that I had anything to offer anyone? Thought that I was bound to be abandoned if I was not the 'best' mother, wife, friend, person I knew? My desperation to please, to make everyone happy, inevitably failed in the hurly burly of life with little ones, simply reinforcing my view of myself as a bad parent.

Those little ones are now young adults, better able to express how they feel, but they are growing up and moving on and I must find a new path; they are not responsible for my well-being. I have a lovely husband who is as supportive as he can be, a sister who keeps me on track, and writing, blogging and going freelance again are all part of a process to take me on through whatever middle-age has in store for me.

Now believe it or not, this is an upbeat story in many ways. I am OK. I have been having counselling for the past year and have come to accept that my various health issues are part of who I am. I am endlessly thankful to the friends and family who love me and, despite how I may feel sometimes, I do enjoy a bloody good laugh, get tipsy and forget myself. I have survived breast cancer for goodness sake, isn't that something to be grateful for? To

4

be proud of? I have learnt how I work best, am most productive and yes happiest. And I understand and believe that I have a right to be happy.

But for me the very best thing, the most positive aspect of all this pain, all the unhappiness I have put myself and my family through is that my James and my Evie have turned out to be confident, caring and as certain as any teenager is about what they want out of life. They are polar opposites of each other – one philosophical and bookish and one sporty and firmly rooted in the here and now – but they are great kids and I am very, very proud of them. I hope my experiences show that however dark the world seems sometimes, however wintry and cold, there is always something to cling to to take you forward. You may struggle for breath but you can get there. And 'there' is where you will find the person you really are.

Dandelions and bad hair days

Vivienne Tufnell

Vivienne Tufnell is the author of the book 'Strangers & Pilgrims' and 'Away with the Fairies' which are both available from Amazon. She blogs regularly at www.zenandtheartoftightropewalking.wordpress.com and has her own website at www.viviennetuffnell.co.uk. Honest and open about her struggles with depressive illness, Vivienne has shared her experiences here in an original and wonderfully creative way. Vivienne also wrote the poem 'Like a cold wind' and the piece 'What depression feels like', also included in this anthology.

A man who took great pride in his lawn found himself with a large crop of dandelions. He tried every method he knew to get rid of them. Still they plagued him. Finally he wrote to the Department of Agriculture. He enumerated all the things he had tried and closed his letter with the question: 'What shall I do now?' In due course the reply came: 'We suggest you learn to love them.'

Anthony de Mello

I've always loved this little story from a great master, but it's taken me years to finally figure out the real meaning.

For a long time, it made me think of my hair. I've got dandelion hair. There are photos of me as a baby with white-blonde hair sticking up like I've had an electric shock, for all the world like a dandelion clock ripe for blowing away. As an adult I have vicious hair, rough like a horse's mane or tail. I've broken many brushes, finding the handle snapping off mid-way through disciplining my mane, or even having a brush disintegrate completely. It's curly enough not to be straight but doesn't wave enough to form proper curls. I have it long because that seemed the simplest way of leaving it; I can do a dozen or more things with it and it's a kind of trademark. But I still envy women with hair that is straight and shiny and that behaves. Mine might go on a psychopathic rampage and throttle people. It's not quite the thing, my hair. About once in 20 or so years pre-Raphaelite hair becomes fashionable and mine suddenly seems the ideal. The rest of the time, it's at best a talking point.

But the dandelions story has become more poignant for me lately as my long-standing depression came roaring back and I've become acutely aware of the years of trying everything to ease it and finding I am without remedy. Over the years I have tried pretty much every medication that was offered, with initial success in terms of alleviating symptoms, which tapered off and then ceased to help. Usually this resulted in taking higher doses, which resulted in increased side effects. I also explored a good number of alternative methods, including exercise, herbal medicine and homoeopathy and even some counselling. I tried energy medicines, flower essences, crystals and pretty much everything wacky and wonderful. Most things worked for a while and then stopped. It's analogous to different ways of dealing with a lawn full of dandelions. You can mow the lawn and cut off the flowers, but three days later they'll be back. You can use a weed-killer that kills off both flowers and leaves, but only the most toxic of weed-killers reach the roots and will leave your soil sterile for years, before the new seeds blow into the garden and start the process again. You can even dig up the entire lawn and try to remove each root by hand (I've actually done this with a new vegetable garden, taking away barrow-loads of roots) but leave even a fraction of root and the whole plant will regenerate. Whatever method you use, the dandelions will eventually grow back.

In terms of my psyche, those dandelions are the symptoms of my depression and they are growing from the very ground of my being. Do I really want to poison my system with mental weed-killers, wipe out and sterilise my psyche by radical treatment like ECT or some of the powerful psychoactive medications? Or spend years digging over and eradicating every root I can find with major psychotherapy (not that this is an economically viable option) only to have new shoots spring up to start the whole cycle again as new seeds settle into the fertile and well tilled soil?

No. It may be time for a new approach, one that is based on acceptance. Those depression-dandelions are growing out of my soul and they're growing to tell me something I surely need to know and I've been unable to face my whole life though.

I'll leave the conclusion to the words of De Mello:

'I too had a lawn I prided myself on and I too was plagued with dandelions that I fought with every means in my power. So learning to love them was no easy matter. I began talking to them each day. Cordial. Friendly. They maintained a sullen silence. They were smarting from the war I had waged against them and were suspicious of my motives.

But it wasn't long before they smiled back. And relaxed. Soon we were good friends.

My lawn, of course, was ruined. But how attractive my garden became!'

Go Wild, Stay Well, Run Hard

Dave Urwin

Dave Urwin describes himself as 'a bearded man from Somerset who occasionally battles depression and anxiety'. He has had a blog on his depression published on the national Mind website and has been interviewed for Positive News. Dave completed his first 50 mile Ultra marathon in February 2012, and is currently training to be a counsellor.

I was lucky to get Dave to slow down long enough to write about his experience of mental ill-health and the amazing way he has found to work at his recovery. He tests his body and mind, raising thousands of pounds for mental health charities Mind and Mind Taunton & West Somerset (Mind TWS) and was instrumental in the establishment of the Mind TWS Ecotherapy project 'Go Wild Stay Well.

'Those who say it cannot be done should not interrupt the ones who are doing it.'

This quote is taken from a runner, Jo, who I've never met but who inspires me beyond belief. Recently he decided to run across Spain; an ambition he'd held for some time, but this year he actually went and did it.

My name's Dave, and throughout my whole life I've struggled with low self-esteem and depression. There are many reasons for this, a lot of which I worked out with my counsellor this year, many more I'm probably still not even aware of, and may never be. These feelings I think are different for everyone, and you have to find your own way to manage them. These are three of the main things that help me...

First in order to be well, you have to strike a balance between looking after others and looking after yourself. Do too much of the former and if it doesn't go both ways, you will burn yourself out. Do too much of the latter without any of the former and life may seem a little hollow. I'm still working on finding the right balance.

Second, it's ok to not be ok. By this I mean that naturally there will be events in life that will not be to your liking; you're only human, and if you feel sad you shouldn't beat yourself up about it. Don't try and fight it; accept it, allow yourself the time and space to process it and in time it's more than likely that you will feel better. Happiness and sadness are not constant states; they are just different parts of who you are. Of course the ideal state is for the former to outweigh the latter, but there are bound to be times when this is not the case. Think of it like seasons. Summer will fade, but it will come back again. Winter will arrive, but it won't stay forever.

Third, there is little that cannot be solved with a nice, long run (or walk).

Let me expand on point three. One day in early April this year I was so depressed that I was unable to concentrate on anything at all. I decided I might as well go for a run, because it might give me a little respite from how I was feeling. Within just a couple of miles the edge had been taken off things; everything that was troubling me in my daily life had been put to one side. It was just me and the outdoors, and my only focus was to keep moving forward. I didn't want to stop. To cut a long story short, I eventually went on to complete 27 miles; just over a full marathon. Admittedly, after about 15 miles, proper running became less and less of a possibility and towards the end it was something of an ungainly stagger, but on that day I learnt a crucial lesson.

Of course, this is not a lesson that is always remembered. There are times when life seems to have dealt me another poor hand, and it seems easier to believe that I'm a woefully inept person and that my life has no purpose, but my counsellor Josephine taught me to think rationally and my first marathon taught me that maybe nothing is out of reach. These lessons are always there, waiting to be rediscovered, and having learnt them I feel better equipped to fight my demons than I ever have before.

I like to think that several others may have learnt similar lessons during the 'Walk on the Wild Side' challenge this year. This was a walking challenge on the Quantocks that I organised to raise funds for Mind in Taunton and West Somerset's 'Go Wild, Stay Well' project, which enables people experiencing mental distress to feel the therapeutic benefits of nature by taking part in conservation work on several stunning nature reserves in the Quantock and Blackdown Hills. There were 16 participants, five of whom joined me for the whole 30 miles. Another 11 joined us half way through to complete 15 miles. Every single one of them completed the challenge, and a number who had completed the 15 mile walk said they would want to do 30 if it was on next year, despite having expressed real reservations about their ability to walk 15 miles before the event. Four of the participants from the 30 mile walk had never walked anywhere near that far in a day before, but all were successful through sheer determination, and through the wonderful sense of camaraderie and humour within the group.

So, this brings me onto my own astronomical endeavour. I'm not going to run across Spain, or England, or even Liechtenstein (well ok, that wouldn't even be a full marathon) but let me explain...

A chain of events has occurred, during which I found out that if one per cent of the UK's population donated 50 pence to any given cause it would raise £30,000......or so I thought! It turns out that my incredibly sloppy mathematical processes meant that I didn't bother to check this calculation, which was wrong – it would actually raise £300,000. I think the only way I can retain any dignity from this appalling mathematical mistake is to actually try and make it happen.

This year I've run a number of events, including a 32 mile ultra marathon on the Jurassic Coast, and will next run the Somerset Levels and Moors marathon on 10th September 2011 (my 30th birthday). I literally will not stop until the target has been met.

I have set up a page on bmycharity.com that can take donations of this amount – it may seem like an awful lot of effort putting in all your details online to donate 50 pence (and there is no obligation to do so of course) but Mind is a fabulous charity and Mind in Taunton & West Somerset would benefit hugely from one 50 pence when combined with other 50 pences from anyone who has one to spare. I really believe this could be a superb way of fundraising – it's not going to break the bank for anyone, but the results really could be astronomically amazing.

I leave you with this final thought; why not think of something you've wanted to do for a long time that you could achieve if you just went ahead and did it? Go ahead and do it. If you don't feel better for having done so I will change my name by deed poll to Uncle Balthazaar.

The Law of Sod, by Chris Rugg

I need to talk, not text talk, not cyber talk, not telephone talk, but face-to-face talk,

I need to feel the presence, hear the reply, to sense the mood,

I need to see the eyes, the lips, the face, hands and body talk,

Then why today of all days is there no one, not a soul to talk to!!

Why? Because family, friends and confidantes live their own lives,

They are planets in my universe, as I am but one planet in theirs,

So, until our orbits coincide, I shall have to wait,

Oh, Bugger, that bloody damnable Law of Sod!!

Moments of truth' in mental health – Lucy's story

Lucy Nicholls

Lucy Nicholls lives in Somerset and works for a patient organisation, helping patients and carers to have their say about health and social care. Hers is a thought provoking and inspirational piece about how brief moments in our lives can take us into chaos, or set us on the path to recovery.

Recently I was looking at some reports about 'chaotic' families in social care. The average 'chaotic family' in Somerset costs the state nearly £200,000 per year. In order to look deeper into these statistics, the people themselves have been asked to talk about their life journeys. During their stories, certain significant moments jump out as turning points. Stepping through the doors of these crucial moments, the families involved started taking destructive paths that ended up in chaos, depression, poverty and dependence. The researchers call these turning-points – in oddly spiritual language – 'moments of truth'.

Reading these stories made me wonder how mental health survivors would tell their own stories. Could this teach us something about successful recovery? Could mental health services create positive 'moments of truth' in order to improve people's lives? Having worked in mental health, I would often look at the people engaged in activities in day services and feel somewhat despairing: surely we can do better in creating turning-points for people?

I consider myself to be a 'survivor'. At the age of 20 I was diagnosed as bi-polar. Coming from a family with a history of mental health problems, I was submitted to a regime of medications: haloperidol, propanolol, prozac, diazepam, lofepramine, thioridazine. Anti-depressants and anti-psychotics: a familiar story of madness. And yet I recovered, as do many people after an episode of severe psychological problems. What were my moments of truth?

I believe my moments partly stemmed from my own horror at 'hitting the bottom': waking up naked in my own garden in the tide of some new medication, being confronted with a cheque but unable to sign my own name, having to pick medication up every couple of days from the pharmacy because I wasn't trusted not to gobble it all up. Those moments made me hate my medication and, in the end, I stopped taking everything except for sedatives.

But more positively, my recovery began with my ninth 'talking therapist' – a psychotherapist called Teresa, who I saw at least once a week for just over two years. She was still, quiet, penetrating and non-judgemental. And I remember that after my first session, after she had said almost nothing while I talked, as I put my hand on the door handle to leave she simply said: 'You are not as mad as you think you are.' No one had told me that before. I had been told: 'You are bi-polar/you are psychotic/you are not to be trusted with your own recovery.' With Teresa's simple statement, my recovery began.

There were other moments of truth, too: a job, a new place to live, a supportive partner, and siblings who helped me, practically and emotionally. But whenever I think of my own recovery, I think of that moment in north London, my hand on the door handle, and Teresa's simple statement whirling through me like a prophecy.

Can we engineer moments of truth, or are they different for each person? Are they, as the language suggests, more spiritual than practical? How do other survivors recall their own recovery – what helps, and what doesn't? And can this inform how we run services for mental health users? Are we offering the right services? Are we making the right moments of truth?

On sense, sensibility & living with an anxious family

Jo Middleton

Jo Middleton is a freelance writer and marketing consultant. She lives in Bristol with her partner and two daughters, where she enjoys alternating between playing hyper-competitive netball and sitting on the sofa watching 30 Rock and eating sweets.

Jo looks at mental health issues from the perspective of someone living with and caring for family members with anxiety and depression. She writes eloquently of her efforts to prevent herself turning into her mother and although most of us have that thought at some point in our lives, for Jo it has different implications.

Read more of Jo's humorous and thought provoking writing on her blog at http://slummysinglemummy.wordpress.com/

Mental ill-health has always been a defining part of my family. Perhaps not in an extreme way, more as background music. My gran experienced depression and anxiety, but of course you didn't call it that then, you just got on with things and suppressed any difficult feelings with plenty of strict routines and good honest hard work.

My mother inherited her mother's depressive tendencies, and was quite profoundly affected by an incident with a bee when she was about 15. My gran was stung, had a reaction, and I think had to be taken to hospital. My mother became terrified of the same thing happening to her, of her throat closing up and of not being able to breathe, and began to have panic attacks.

Unable to talk about her feelings with a mother whose answer to everything was to produce a large meal with a high fat content, she has struggled with her anxiety ever since. The panic attacks continued, and many a night as a child I was woken up by my mum pleading with me to call her an ambulance as she couldn't breathe, and was sure she was dying.

My sister, who is four years younger than me, also has the family anxiety gene, and spent much of her early childhood at home with my mum, unwilling or unable to go to school, certain that the local nuclear power station was about to explode at any moment.

From quite a young age then, I became the sensible, organised, happy one in the family, often tasked with 'cheering up my sister'. I never resented this, and was always happy to come up with some kind of interesting activity for us both. I use the word 'interesting' in the loosest possible sense

– one of our favourite games was 'Estate Agents'. Always looking to get out of the house, my mum would quite often pretend to be wealthy, and spend afternoons looking around large properties for sale. In the process, my sister and I would collect house details, tippex out the company headers, and replace them with our own. We'd then set up our bedroom as an office, and pass the time taking imaginary phone calls and making appointments for viewings. Happy days.

The idea I'm interested in though, is to what extent the roles we are assigned as children shape our personalities as adults. I don't doubt that my experiences as a child, and the experiences I continue to have as an adult, have a profound effect on how I see myself, and my place in the world.

This, of course, can be both positive and negative. Living with people who tend to worry, and who see the first signs of meningitis in every stiff neck or headache, has forced me to look on the bright side of life, to try to see the positive in things. My way of rebelling against my parents is to be eternally cheerful and optimistic. This means I'm normally pretty laid back, take things in my stride, and like to live in the moment. I don't really do long-term planning and I tend not to worry too much about the consequences of my actions. I like to have fun, but it can be messy, and results in a lot of hangovers.

On the down side, I do sometimes feel an exaggerated sense of responsibility to other people, a desire to live up to my role as 'the sensible one'. An ex-boyfriend once described me as 'cold-hearted' and, although it stung at the time, I think there is an element of truth. It's not that I don't care; it's just that years of caring have forced me to toughen up, to take a step back from my emotions. To me, being over-emotional is a weakness and I don't like to be seen as weak. I don't like to feel things too deeply. Being positive has become a reflex – feeling anxious or worried about something? Don't! Just think of something happy, quick!

What this also means is that if I ever experience instances of depression or anxiety, it terrifies me. The prospect of long-term depression or anxiety is far scarier than the reality of it. No one wants to turn into their mother after all.

So what do you think? How do our experiences of mental ill-health as a child shape us as adults and to what extent do we find ourselves defined by the roles we are assigned when we are young?

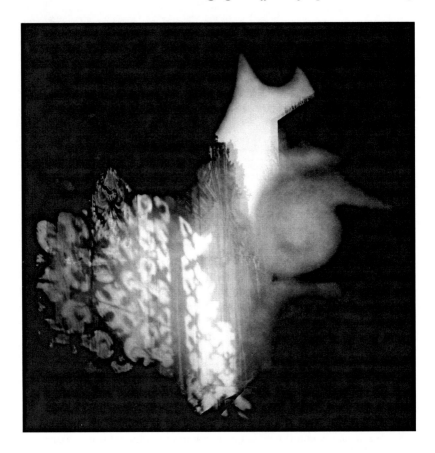

Depression isn't the end of the world; it just feels like it...

Stephanie Matthews

Stephanie is a 44-year-old working in the legal profession. She has suffered from severe bouts of depression since her late teens. She is now happily married with a young daughter and is qualified as a Flower Remedies therapist, aromatherapist and crystal healer. She is still taking medication for her mental health. Here she has felt able to share her experience as a woman, wife and mother living with depression. She has been to the edge and she writes frankly of her experience of admission to a psychiatric inpatient unit and how, after her discharge, it inspired her to take control to ensure she never had to return.

I've suffered with periodic bouts of depression since my late teens. I'm now in my early 40s so that's nearly 30 years of feeling like my world is about to cave in at any moment. It hasn't yet, and now after all this time, I'm starting to believe that it never will.

In 1998 I had just come out of an acrimonious break up with a long-term boyfriend. I'd lost a lot of weight and spent my days pretty much on autopilot. I was living on rice, chickpeas and black coffee and my already stressful job was made worse by the fact that my ex worked in an office just along the corridor to mine. One evening, after going out and getting very drunk, I emptied the bathroom cabinet and took every pill I could find until I passed out. My flatmate found me and rang an ambulance. I woke up in hospital the following day with a very sore throat and a stomach full of charcoal because they hadn't managed to pump it properly.

All I can really remember of that time is a vision of a deep pit where the blackness is thick and cloying and slowly suffocates you because you can't get out. I was discharged from hospital with just a prescription for antidepressants. No follow-up appointment, no counselling, nothing. But already I was labelled, and consequently judged. I had tried to kill myself. I was mentally unstable. I was mad.

I retrained and changed jobs. The depression was manageable. I'd come off the antidepressants and was treating myself with St Johns Wort. I'd started doing yoga to help deal with the stress and I'd stopped trying to fit into an uncomfortable mould and started to be a little more – 'me'. Most important of all I'd stopped drinking. I enjoyed work. I had a social life. I'd got through some extremely stressful episodes – the death of my father, redundancy, moving house, getting married. I made the mistake of thinking I was cured.

All that changed when my daughter was born in 2006. After four miscarriages and an utterly horrendous pregnancy which culminated in gestational diabetes and pre-eclampsia, we endured a very difficult birth. Surprisingly, she has proved to be an extremely happy, healthy and stable child.

I, on the other hand, descended rapidly into post-natal depression, sleep deprivation, hallucinations and psychosis. When I finally admitted to my health visitor that I had actually thought about killing myself and my daughter, the mental health team were called in. I was put forward for CBT, but there was no funding available – and besides, by this time, the financial reality was that I had to go back to work. I was put on different antidepressants and sent on my way. So I muddled on, knowing that I was slowly sliding deeper into the pit that I couldn't get out of and feeling increasingly incapable of coping with a boisterous, growing, intelligent and startlingly normal child.

In May 2010, it fell apart again. I collapsed one Sunday night feeling like the mirror that was my mind had shattered into a million glittering pieces. I couldn't do anything except cry. I couldn't talk to my boss, my mother, my husband. My GP put me on a higher dose of citalopram and signed me off for a month. He referred me for counselling but warned me that there was a nine-month waiting list. I tried to glue the pieces together and went back to work.

In August, after a row with my best friend, I told my husband that I was going to take all the paracetamol I could find because I just couldn't live like that any longer. I was utterly exhausted, mentally in pieces and wishing I was somewhere – anywhere – else. The next thing I knew, I was sitting in an interview room in my local mental health unit being told they had found me a bed. I was being admitted for my own safety.

Being an inpatient was both a terrifying and a revelatory experience. Although the wards were segregated, the canteen was not, and I suffered severe panic attacks every time I had to go for a meal. Otherwise, during the day I almost never saw anyone apart from the staff when they did their 15-minute checks. It took 48 hours to get used to not being allowed to go anywhere alone, having to tell a nurse where I was going at all times, having doors locked behind me, asking permission to make a phone call. But it taught me that I could take control of my life, and find a way of sorting my illness out so I never ever have to come back again.

Before I was discharged, my drugs were changed again, to mirtazapine and boy did I notice the difference! I ate everything, slept for hours at a time and felt like I had cotton wool in my head. I also had no control over my temper, throwing things at my husband for no reason, totally misinterpreting everything he said and did. I begged the CPN to change my meds, but they put the dosage up and gave me tranquillisers for the times when the rage or panic got too much. I immediately telephoned a dear friend and homeopath in desperation, and she made up a homoeopathic remedy from the mirtazapine which I now take instead. As she is also a counsellor, she is helping me with that too, since the NHS has only just reached my name on the waiting list!

Things are now better. I am no longer working. The job is just soul-destroying and I can do well without the stress at the moment. Financially it was a very poor decision, but perhaps I should have done it years before and saved myself all this trouble. I am retraining again, studying to become a naturopath. I am slowly finding alternative ways of making an income and am evangelising 'Make Do and Mend'. I have finally got counselling through the NHS, although still no CBT. And I'm off my meds.

My mental state, though, is still fragile. I can't cope with stress very well and large crowds still make me panic. But I can run a house, make decisions and play with my daughter. I know people still judge me because at best people think I'm a skiving whinger (and yes, I have been called that to my face) or at worst deluding myself into thinking that I'm not mad when, of course, I am.

Depression is an illness. Same as diabetes, cancer, high blood pressure. It has the potential to kill you if you don't do anything about it. It is capable of crippling you, leaving you unable to function at the most basic level. Unlike diabetes, cancer or high blood pressure though, you can't take a photo of it or check it with basic tests. A photo of my brain wouldn't show you anything, but believe me, the illness is there. I don't think I'll ever be free of it, but I know I can manage it and I know I can live with it.

Depression may not be my best friend but it is no longer my enemy. Of late it has taught me a great deal about myself and what is really, truly, deeply important to me. And the biggest lesson it's taught is that life, with all its faults and flaws, really is worth living.

Underneath the Lemon Tree - an interview with Mark Rice-Oxley

Mark Rice-Oxley is an assistant news editor on the foreign desk of The Guardian newspaper. Seeming to 'have it all' - great job, marriage, children- he was as surprised as everyone around him when he succumbed to a serious depression that he has recently described in vivid detail in his book 'Underneath the Lemon Tree'. Mark kindly agreed to break from a hectic schedule of book promotion to answer a few questions about his experiences.

Could you give me a brief description of the life you were living before you became ill?

I was a hyper-busy working father with three small children, a full-time job, freelance commitments and an amateur musician. We had three children (and one miscarriage) in five years, so I like to reflect on five years, four pregnancies, three kids, two jobs (regular and freelance), one wife and no life.

Before you experienced depression first hand, what was your view of those with mental health issues? Do you think those views were from a particularly 'male' perspective? (i.e. the need to be strong etc.)

For me, depression was for other people. I simply didn't have time for it. And I thought as I had nothing to be sad about that I would be immune. I didn't realise that depression is also bound up in stress, adrenalin and overexertion - in essence, it's the body's way of getting a very important message through. And I got the message, loud and clear.

I don't think I approached this from a particularly 'male' angle. I'm not a very blokey bloke and was actually quite surprised when I learned that three times as many women as men 'present' with depression.

How have those views changed?

I'm a bit of an evangelist now. Prevention is better than cure. I can see men all around me carrying on as if they have some kind of god-like immunity, and I want to say to them 'read a few chapters of my book and rethink your life.' I will always be prone to this illness now. But if only others can be made aware, they can stop themselves before it's too late.

Reading the prologue to 'Underneath the Lemon Tree' it is clear that depression hit you in a very physical way. When did you first realise something was seriously wrong?

I was aware in September 2009 that something was definitely not right, but I didn't know what it was. It was physical - lethargy, mild panic, early waking, headaches - but nothing so urgent that you could use it to persuade others (my family, my GP) that something was amiss. It wasn't until my birthday weekend in October 2009 that it became absolutely unignorable.

You have tried a number of treatments in the past two years, with more or less success; but from a medical or psychotherapeutic perspective what do you think has helped you most?

It's hard to say because you try half a dozen things all at once and are not too sure which has helped the most. But for me, meditation, acceptance and curiosity have been the holy trinity, and psychotherapy helped me to understand that. Meditation/mindfulness because it stops you getting carried away and slipping back into old frenetic habits; acceptance because you can't struggle against this or you make it worse; and curiosity because I've needed to work out why I am the way that I am in order to change things and prevent relapse. The other tactics which helped with the symptoms (if not the cause) included: medication, exercise, gentle socialising, time, love, patience and, yes, writing!

Clearly you adore your family and I know that I have always worried about how my anxiety and depression affects my husband, children, mother and sister. Have you been able to talk to those closest to you about how they coped with caring for you during your darkest times?

My wife and I have always shared everything; we have talked so much about this and not just about me, but about how it affected her. We've also had short sessions with the children, who can be quite perspicacious despite their years. My eight-year-old asked me the other day: 'How did you look after us when you were ill?' I found that hard to answer.

It isn't long since your breakdown (although I understand that is not a term doctors use anymore it is clear you felt, as I have, 'broken' in some way) - was writing this book part of your 'recovery' process or did you have other reasons for setting everything out so explicitly?

Writing is therapy. It always has been for me. It is the way we bring order to a chaotic world, and there's nothing more chaotic than the mind when it is on the blink. But there were other reasons for writing: I hunted for a book like this early in my illness, seeking reassurance and instruction on what I could expect. I wanted to write a book for people descending into this illness in 2012. I also wanted to create a talking point. I believe mental illness is a bit like homosexuality in the 1950s - a shameful secret that most of us keep hidden. This plainly doesn't help - sufferers need to be open in order to recover and society needs to understand this scourge a lot better than it does.

I would describe much of your writing as poetic and at times you seem almost to pour your feelings onto the page. As a journalist have you always had that creative approach to writing or is this something you discovered as you wrote this book? Do you feel you want to do more of this type of work now?

Although I am a journalist, I have rarely had the chance to write creatively like this. News writing is a science, not an art, and it's often frustrating to be limited to 700 words. I think some of that frustration, built up over 20 years, came tumbling out during 'lemon tree'; I do have a poetic sensibility, can hear the beauty in the cadence of words and have always had a fascination for the different modes of expression. Sometimes short sentences work. Sometimes you feel the need to be more lyrical. I do very much hope to write again, but hopefully next time it won't be about me.

And finally, can you give me the background to your book's haunting title, 'Underneath the Lemon Tree'?

The lemon tree was my trusty companion throughout the ordeal. We felt the image was bang on and the metaphor worked nicely too. I'm kind of sorry about the way it all turned out (the lemon tree died, despite the care given to it), but c'est la vie.

'Underneath the Lemon Tree: a Memoir of Depression and Recovery' by Mark Rice-Oxley was published in March 2012 by Little Brown

With or without Words

Anna Colgan

Anna is a Core Process Psychotherapist and SE (Somatic Experiencing) practitioner. She came to psychotherapy after a career in teaching through her own experience of stress and distress, and believes passionately in the power of body orientated psychotherapy to help heal our early wounding. Anna was trained at the famous Karuna Institute and works in the South West, using an approach based on Buddhist and Western influences. Find out more at www.annacolgan.co.uk

I have an interview with Occupational Health and the doctor is trying to help me out: 'Can't sleep, can't eat?'

'Oh, no, I can eat and sleep', I say, and wish I hadn't. Will he stop my sick pay if I can eat and sleep? Does he have a tick list of symptoms of human distress? Perhaps I should just have agreed with him. I can't tell him how I do feel; it won't go into words.

I knew I felt fine when I was busy preparing for friends coming to stay and not fine after they'd gone. I knew some people would say the answer was to keep busy, but no-one can keep busy for twenty four hours a day every day of their lives. How did I feel when I was not fine? I felt uncomfortable, like I wanted to cry but I couldn't, like I wanted to howl, like I wanted to get something out. Maybe I should have said that to the doctor in the interview.

All conversations on the subject seem so difficult. Some weeks before when I was first signed off, I rang the Deputy Head; he was concerned for me because our Head didn't take kindly to teachers who were off with stress. I think our Head thought that if you were stressed you were doing the job properly. So I told the Deputy Head that it was just me, I had depression, nothing to do with work.

So why do I feel so much better now that I'm not at work?

My GP saw that I was not well enough to continue to teach because when I tried to talk to him about it I burst into tears in his consulting room. I was lucky: my body spoke its mind.

Eventually I have to see the psychiatrist who will either confirm or deny what my GP has decided; that I am not well enough to go to back to my job. By this time I am training to be a psychotherapist, so now my worry is that the psychiatrist will think I know enough to convincingly present as a person who is not well enough to work. But what can I do? I have to be me, and by now me is someone who is training to be a psychotherapist. I tell him, 'I don't think I was listened to as a child. And now I can't cope with the kids sometimes not listening when I'm trying to teach.' I wonder if he will ask me why anyone who wants to be listened to would choose secondary teaching as a profession, but he doesn't. Thankfully he seems to have the imagination to encompass cumulative stress, so it is coherent that for over twenty years I was fine, combative and cheerful around naughty teenagers, and now I'm not. I relax; he is reflecting back to me that my story makes sense.

One friend on the phone says, 'This has gone on long enough; you should get anti-depressants.' I say they would just cover over the feelings, like alcohol would. But my friend says that is not an analogy. I consult my Alexander Technique teacher who counsels against my taking anti-depressants. She says that my system is very sensitive; she knows because Alexander lessons brought out the most searing depression, or emotional pain, or whatever you call it, that had been held in my spine. And I was always glad that this had happened; I never regretted this, never wished it had stayed in. But it was not easy to live through it. I can't tell my friend that depression has come out of my spine; she will think I have become a hippy.

I spend a few years working at Mind, and see people whose depression is so painful, as they sit facing me I see that their distress is like an undershirt of barbed wire between their skin and their clothes. Sometimes people say they can't go on like this. One day, as part of my training, I work-shadowed the very psychiatrist who had been so perceptive in my case, and he sits with someone I perceive to be in this state, but he dismisses this man and says, 'I don't think he is depressed'. We see different things.

My psychotherapy training is rigorous so I am in personal therapy for years; therapists reflect back to me so more and more of my story makes sense. I continue with various approaches such as Alexander and cranio-sacral and more pain is released.

My training is body based psychotherapy and my body is given many chances to speak its mind, and it speaks volumes. It listens too; now I listen with my body to my clients.

The value of friendship

Chris Rugg

Friendship is a strange and mysterious mutual feeling of trust, support and affection between two people. You cannot see it, yet you can perceive it; you cannot touch it, yet you can feel it; you cannot hear it, yet you can sense it. It is as essential to our wellbeing as breathing; it is a natural selective bond which forms and grows with some of the people we meet, but by no means all. It is certainly as strong as love and is very often stronger. It is a gift which cannot be valued too highly.

Depression, the clinical kind, is a mental disorder which affects many millions of people of every race, class and religion; no one is immune from it. For those affected, depression has an absolutely devastating effect, not only on their lives but on the lives of their families and loved ones. It is also life-threatening and the feeling of failure after an unsuccessful suicide attempt is inexpressible.

Like many life-changing events depression acts as a 'filter of friends'; it is only when you are really ill or in need that you find out who your true friends are, if indeed any! It will be found that many people regarded as friends slowly drift away until they are seen no more. This has much to do with the stigma associated with mental illness, and the stereotypical image of mental illness. In the end there are few very good friends left and, because of the depression and the fact that they are good friends, you deliberately see them less and less, trying not to be a burden on them; eventually they feel shunned and drift away.

As stated earlier on, friendship is essential to our wellbeing, so even though depressed, new friendships begin to form, many of them are with others who have, or have had mental health problems. These are not temporary friendships or friendships of convenience, they are deep and meaningful friendships that will last a lifetime, no matter what happens. These are friendships born out of shared experience and a mutual willingness to help one another get through the bad times, no matter how hard things may be.

This gift of friendship is an essential ingredient in the treatment of all kinds of mental disorder, not only depression. Although I am not a believer in the current buzz-word 'recovery' when applied to depression, I do believe that friendship gives the ability and will to lead a more open and balanced life. And if, as is often the case, you slide back into another episode of depression, you know that your new-found friends are there and that they will do all they can to help you.

Loneliness, by Mark Kelly

Like a cancer it starts, unseen, unfelt, unwanted
Deep within the darkest recesses of the soul it grows, festers
Little by little it expands, corrupting, ruining all that it touches
Slowly it eats away at your very being, as yet undetected
Subtle changes start in your life but you go on
Paying little heed to the signs of the coming storm

It builds, constructing a web of destruction from within
Life proceeds. Unaware of the constant change, unseen
Energy wanes, interest fades, life contracts, an ever decreasing world
A withdrawal from participation, interaction, contact
An island in the ocean that is life, solitary, singular, alone
Uncaring, unmotivated, withdrawn, solitude your only comfort

Some notice, few comment, most too involved to respond
Too involved to care or, perhaps, fighting their own battle within
Is it you? Is it the world? Is it life itself?
A path to self-destruction, crowded but without company, alone
Is the whole world on the same path, with hate and ignorance the theme?
Focussed on the degrading, destructive, petty, caring little for life and hope

Are you so far out of touch with reality? Not understanding this modern
world
Anarchy, hate, despair, anger, greed, selfishness, destruction
These seem to rule, but it's a world you cannot accept
So you disconnect, withdraw into an internal fortress of solitude
Dismissing contact, friendship, companions, love
A social circle of one, living in a world of darkness, alone

But inside the need builds, fighting the web of loneliness that holds tight
Though without the drive to break free, almost crushed
Needs and wants forgotten, buried deep by despair and fear
Fear of what? The unknown? The world? Life?
Perhaps none, perhaps all, you don't care, don't want to know
It has utter control now, you just want to be....alone

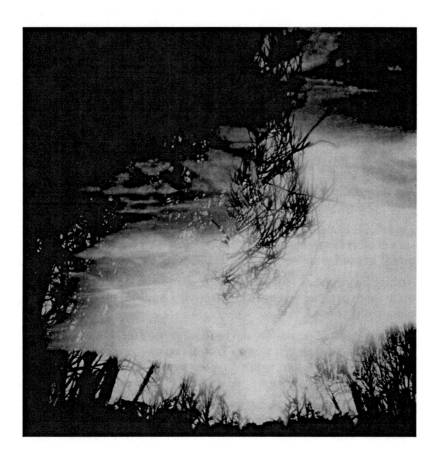

Naming the Beast

Rin Simpson

Rin Simpson is a freelance journalist and creative writer, and the founder of The Steady Table writers' group (@TheSteadyTable). Born in South Africa, she moved to the UK when she was 14 and is now based in Bristol. As well as writing she loves crafts of all kinds but particularly knitting, and has permanently itchy feet, which have taken her from Japan and Thailand to Zambia and Morocco, and beyond. Interestingly, Rin does not consider herself to suffer from depression - it's just something she has to deal with every now and then. Nonetheless, she writes movingly of her battles with it and how she believes it is vital to take control of your own recovery. You can read Rin's blog at www.nowiamthirty.journoblog.net.

Have you ever had a day where you feel so angry or sad or otherwise negative that you feel like your head might explode, but you just can't quite figure out why?

As the hours go by the anger or the sadness are joined by other feelings – guilt at having snapped at your children, shame at having burst into tears on your boss, fear that you're going crazy.

And then you have a light bulb moment: of course, you're due on in a couple of days, you've just got PMT!

The relief is immediate. Sure you might still be snappy and weepy and all sorts of other things, but at least now you know what you're dealing with, even if it is still meddling with your emotional wellbeing.

Nothing is ever quite as frightening when you turn on the light and face it out in the open rather than listen to it scurrying around in the darkest corners of your mind.

The same is true of depression, and that's why one of the things I most despise about the disease is the way it sneaks up on you without announcing its true nature, so that for a few days or weeks or even months you live in fear.

Fear that you're going crazy, that you're a bad person, that you're simply not good enough because suddenly things that you were managing to hold together just fine – a job, a relationship, a normal routine involving doing the dishes and taking off your makeup – seem beyond your grasp.

Depression makes you feel like you can't cope with anything. Your judgement goes completely out of the window, particularly your perceptions about yourself, your worth as a human being and your ability to change.

Or maybe it's just me. That's another problem – the lack of dialogue about the disease, which leaves sufferers isolated and guilt-ridden, feeling that they really ought to just 'pull themselves together', that there are people with far worse problems and that they are just being weak and lazy and self-obsessed.

All of this goes on, for me, under the surface for an indefinite period of time. After all, you can't let your crazy show, can you? You've got a job to hold down, kids to take care of, stuff to do, for goodness sake. You can't afford to have a meltdown and anyway, what would people think?

So you cope (and I use the word loosely) for as long as possible. But in time cracks start to show and eventually you come to the end of yourself, to the point where you simply can't anymore.

And it's often around then that you have that light bulb moment I was talking about: of course, I'm not going crazy; I'm experiencing a bout of depression!

That's when you can stop blaming yourself for how you're feeling, or for not dealing with things better, recognise that you have a disease and get on with the healing process.

Blame makes you feel trapped, not least because if you feel like something is your fault then you'll probably be too ashamed to ask for help. If you can identify the problem, you can start to shake off the blame.

I am a firm believer that those who suffer from depression have to play a part in our own healing. Just as we can't blame ourselves, we equally cannot simply blame the disease for all our problems and wallow in the unfairness of it all.

But it's vital to recognise that depression is a disease, and identify it as quickly and accurately as possible – not just the first time it strikes, but every time. Only then can healing begin. Only then can we start to hope again for the future.

Why?--A Complex Tragedy

Lois Chaber

Born a New Yorker, Lois Chaber was absorbed in a conventional academic career as a scholar/teacher in 18th-Century English Literature until she was lured away to the Middle East in the mid-1970s by her third husband, a dynamic New Zealander. There they experienced first-hand the turbulent triumph of Islamic fundamentalism in this oil-rich region and eventually left with Sybil and her younger sister Molly for London, where Lois has taught for a decade in a small American university. Various family misfortunes reached their climax in 1999 with Sybil's tragic suicide, which compelled Lois to begin her memoir. A life-long anxiety/depression sufferer, Lois presently benefits from psychotropic medicine, Quaker meetings, good literature, purring cats, the Jane Fonda Workout, and many rewarding relationships. She is committed to supporting various mental health charities. At the end of the piece Lois includes full details of where you can obtain her moving memoir 'The Thing Inside My Head': A Family's Journey through Mental Illness' published by Chipmunka Publishing.

My daughter, Sybil Macindoe, suffered so severely from Obsessive-Compulsive Disorder (OCD) and related mental illnesses that in 1999 she took her own life. People with OCD experience distressing, intrusive thoughts, often relating to fears of harm to themselves or others. In a futile attempt to reduce these very uncomfortable anxieties, they engage in compulsive rituals such as excessive hand-washing and repeated checking. In November, 1996, Sybil wrote this poem:

Oh why did it go wrong? Why?

I must be strong.

Sometimes I want to write out my whole story,

but I don't have the patience to achieve that glory.

Everything is like an instant in my mind,

An explosion where you can see everything, all my troubles

Going up in the air for one second

Then it falls and becomes muck and rubble.

I have so much I'm carrying inside me,

But I fumble in the dark

For the door to let it out.

I feel like turning all those pains,

Those memories into a single scream or shout.

Where will I go when I am finished writing?

I am living, putting on a show, for the rest of my life.

When I came across this poem in one of Sybil's diaries - diaries that held often shocking revelations kept secret from her family until after her death - I felt compelled to write a book that would attempt to answer her question,'Why'? In the process I increasingly realised that the cause(s) of mental illness and their repercussions were far more complex and labyrinthine than they are normally figured - by the average man/woman in the street, by the media, and - yes! - even by the NHS. Sybil's 'whole story' was intimately bound up with my own psychic struggle and with the trials of our family members, both individually and collectively, in five different countries. The connections between our family difficulties and Sybil's illness were something I strove to articulate in the book, which is subtitled 'A Family's Journey Through Mental Illness'. Sybil's fate was also profoundly affected by the strengths and the shortcomings of the successive counsellors and institutions that tried to help her and which proved to be a learning curve for our family, one which I wanted to share with those faced with running the gauntlet of the mental health services.

One of the few NHS personnel who grasped the extraordinarily complex, cumulative nature of the background to Sybil's very severe case was a psychiatric nurse in The Bethlem Royal Adolescent Unit where Sybil spent over two years frustrating all the consultants' theories:

'There was some feeling before that there had been a major trauma, and this was the result of it. I suppose I just didn't really believe that. I think it was a case of a combination of things that had happened. Sybil would often say quite shocking things, like, 'Do you think my father sexually abused me?' And I'd say, 'No, I think what has actually happened and why you find it so hard to talk about it, is that it all seems like nothing'. And one of the things was the family being in Qatar and unable to leave because Neil's passport had been taken away... And it was by her bringing up things like that, that she finally realised we weren't expecting one big disclosure.'

It began at the beginning. Sybil's birth experience was traumatic: seven weeks premature, in a foreign hospital in Tehran, in the midst of the build-up to the Iranian Revolution in 1978, and kept apart from all contact with me for a whole week in an incubator in the Tehran Clinic's neo-natal ward. Additionally, my own untreated mental health problems--chronic depression and anxiety (aggravated by 'the baby blues')--made me an inconsistent carer and a faulty role model throughout Sybil's childhood. Mental illness, when not addressed, can be passed down from generation to generation through a parent's behaviour as well as by genes.

Sybil probably inherited a predisposition to anxiety disorders, but the many difficulties our family experienced as expatriates not only in Iran but in the Arabian Gulf and in Britain (I was born an American, Neil, a New Zealander) were 'triggers' both for the emergence of her problems and their growing severity. Just before Ayatollah Khomeini flew into Tehran, we 'escaped' from Iran to the Gulf State of Qatar, where Sybil and later her sister Molly spent their childhood weekends on sandy beaches dotted with wandering camels, Neil worked on planning and construction projects, and I taught English literature in the sex-separated national university. But even the family dynamics there were working against Sybil. I remained unstable, at one point landing up in hospital after an overdose. Her Qatar-born younger sister Molly, easier for me to cope with and born in less dramatic circumstances, developed into a more outgoing and robust child than Sybil, and this, plus their closeness in age (only a year and a half difference), led to a very pronounced sibling rivalry, as Sybil drew more and more into herself and became increasingly less confident.

On top of that, the Iranian Revolution had encouraged anti-Western bias in some quarters of this Gulf country and Sybil's dad, a construction manager, was made a scapegoat for unpaid company debts by the Qatari owners of his firm. His unjust persecution and the confiscation of his passport profoundly terrified the ultra-sensitive seven-year-old Sybil, and she began to disintegrate. Among her many manifestations, meaningless to us in the mid-1980s, were her refusal to swallow her saliva, which she thought was poison, and her repeated moaning that she 'wished she'd never been born.' Our total ignorance of anything to do with OCD and the lack of an English-speaking child psychiatrist there during this crisis played a large role in determining the subsequent severity of Sybil's illness.

Our ignorance of OCD continued until in 1991, a few years after our resettlement in England, a U.S. friend posted us an article about this newly-highlighted disease. The symptoms perfectly chimed with Sybil's 'eccentricities'. Sybil's strange behaviour and her difficulty making friends had led us in 1987 to seek help from a child guidance clinic. By the 1990s Sybil was washing and praying excessively and endlessly 'repeating things', but the clinicians involved in her case were not prepared to deal with OCD even after we shared our new information with them. Her dad's prolonged unemployment in the 1990s recession brought more stress and explosive tensions for the whole family. Sybil would frequently bolt out of the house shrieking 'Save me Lord' and proclaiming that angels of judgement were coming after her. Unbeknown to us, it was a form of OCD now identified as 'religious scrupulosity'. Sufferers are irrationally convinced they are extreme sinners, requiring punishment (John Bunyan, author of Pilgrim's Progress, experienced amazingly similar symptoms). When her dad had to leave for his only work prospect in Nigeria, Sybil's distress was such that she completely stopped eating, drinking and talking and spent most of the day twisting her body into bizarre postures.

Sybil eventually had to be institutionalised, at the age of 14. In the course of six years, she was to experience two adolescent units, an adolescent therapeutic community and, finally, an adult mental health ward in Essex. Her confused inner torment during the early years of her institutionalisation was only revealed to us by reading, after her death, her written account of her years at the second unit, the Bethlem Royal:

'When I first went to the Bethlem, Mrs Wells, who I had been living with in foster care, drove my mum and I down to the Bethlem. I wasn't eating; I had an ng [nasogastric] tube up my nose. I wasn't talking. I had my head right back as if I was looking up at the ceiling and my eyes rolled right back. I kept my eyes and head like this all the time except for when lying down in bed. I didn't communicate at all except for a sort of smile, which meant agreement or 'yes'. On the second day there my key worker Jane was on shift. That was when I started communicating with ticks, crosses and question marks. Jane suggested it and the thing inside my head which I thought was God said I could do it.'

Sybil's demanding internal 'voice' or 'voices' at times ('God and the Devil') come and go, dominating the diaries we only had access to when it was too late. The main title of my memoir became 'The Thing Inside My Head.'

Sybil's acceptance by her friendly teenage peer group in the Bethlem Royal Unit, within the cheerful, informal environment of the unit, was the primary healing agent enabling her to finally break free from her extreme eating disorder and behavioural paralysis, after two years of the consultants coming up in vain with different successive theories (including a supposition that she'd been sexually abused by her dad). This is why our family strongly believes that young mental health sufferers, even those between 18 and 25 years, benefit greatly from age-related placement. However, her fundamental OCD and her twisted religious misinterpretations went essentially unresolved because the unit felt it was time for her 'to move on' now that she didn't need a naso-gastric tube.

34

And meanwhile, other members of the family were suffering. I was so distressed by Sybil's extreme behaviour, her institutionalisation and my husband's unfortunate but necessary residence in Africa that I had to have thrice-weekly therapy sessions at the Tavistock Centre. My husband, Neil, striving to keep the family afloat economically, felt constant frustration and helplessness at being so far away from the family, from the hospitals where Sybil was an on-going resident, and her younger sister Molly was confused and miserable. Years later Molly confided to me what we were too obsessed with Sybil's plight to perceive at the time:

'I felt a mixture of feelings about going to see her: going was like a duty; staying at home made me feel guilty. Mum and Dad would go on at me and say that I would have a stronger influence on her because I was closer to her age and could bring her out of herself more. ... [But] it was hard when she wasn't communicating. I guess I was just being selfish and not really thinking about her, just being bored there ... Sometimes she was worse and sometimes she was better. My mum tried to explain to me what she had, but I didn't really understand much. I only knew she had mental problems.'

Sybil is a tragic example of why early intervention in the case of genuinely mentally disturbed children is crucial. By the time she finally received appropriate treatment in an adult ward in her later teenage years after an unhappy experience in the therapeutic community with a totally inappropriate peer group of aggressive, abused young persons, her beliefs and behaviours - which included persistent self-harming - were deeply entrenched. Reverend Richard Smith, a trained psychotherapist and senior chaplain to the Healthcare Trust in Essex whose care Sybil was under from age 17 to 20, had become Sybil's confidante, seeing her often. He commented to me after her death (in an interview):

'I have to say to you that I have never met anybody so severely suffering from OCD as Sybil... I tried to create a threat-safe space for Sybil in which she could just be, but my frustration, and to some extent, anger, is that I felt it was too late for me really to be able to do that. I think Sybil had become so severely ill even two years prior to her death that it really limited what kind of relationship I could form with her and what I could do for her ... '

Sybil had blossomed for a while under a programme of ERP (Exposure and Response Prevention), some CBT, and drug therapy--she was living in supported accommodation, starting to catch up educationally and doing voluntary work. But her medication gradually became ineffective, especially when behavioural therapies were discontinued by a high-handed decision from her NHS therapist. This, as well as conflicts in our family (between Neil and me, and between both of us and the rebellious teenager Molly) and strife in her half-way house (between clients and management), led to a relapse and a return to hospital. The final diary we 'inherited' is a register of Sybil's growing despair. Here is a sample:

> 'I don't know what's God's voice & what isn't
>
> HELP
>
> I'M ANGRY
>
> Bedtime: I'm frustrated at the thoughts I'm frustrated because of my behaviour I have to do which then is a nuisance--makes me look strange I look strange in other ways I feel like harming myself I want to die
>
> HELP'

Not long after writing this, Sybil found an opportunity to end her life; there were inadequacies in the ward's physical environment i.e. the absence of collapsible rail curtains, and the ward had decided not to remove her stereo player electrical cord, despite the fact that it had been previously used for a dry run of her tragic 'escape' from despair.

What I've written here is merely a sketch of what Sybil and our family went through. I hope anyone more interested in Sybil's case - especially the insights provided by her raw and often searing diary entries - will have a look at my lengthy memoir and its reviews: 'The Thing Inside My Head': A Family's Journey through Mental Illness, Chipmunka Publishing, IBSN 9781847474018, on Amazon and other online booksellers. All royalties and any other profits go to the specialist charity, OCD Action.

Social media and the blues

Jane Alexander

Jane Alexander is a journalist and the author of over 20 books on health and wellbeing. She is passionate about removing the stigma from mental health – particularly as she has battled with depression herself over many years. She blogs at www.exmoorjane.blogspot.com Here Jane writes candidly about online relationships and the support, or otherwise, that social networking offers to those experiencing mental health issues.

A few weeks ago I fell into one of my bad places...possibly the worst one for a very long time. One of those declines – oh, okay, let's not mince words – was free-fall skydiving without a parachute. At first I couldn't speak. Couldn't get my fingers to type. Couldn't do anything really. As I sat at my desk, doing nothing, I watched social media drift by. And I wondered...what's it all about? What is it all about?

I have always advocated social media as a form of self-help, a kind of informal (and free) therapy. I know for a fact that I use my blog as a way of working out stuff. By writing out our feelings, our thought processes, our angst and our anguish, I do believe we can come to realisations. By watching our reactions to other people we can trudge through our issues with ego, shadow and so on. Equally, if we are writing about our mental health issues, it can be enormously comforting and validating when we get supportive comments. You don't feel so alone; you don't feel like such a freak, such a waste of space. You're not the only person in the world who has post natal depression (PND) or who is bipolar or schizophrenic. You're not the only one whose black dog deserves an ASBO.

I've watched people in anguish being 'caught' (in the rescue kind of way) on Facebook and on Twitter too. Seen them being talked down from self-harming or even life-threatening situations and it has left me in awe of the kindness of strangers. For, remember, these are not our real life friends and family but chance connections on the web. The cynic in me says that some will simply love the drama, will want to be part of the do-good crowd. Fake love-bombing is a horrible thing. But many are totally genuine and some will go the extra mile. Angels. Seriously.

But you have to reach out in the first place. And sometimes, oh sometimes, you just can't. Then, see, social media can be the loneliest place in the whole universe that exists inside your head-space. When you're way down low, when you're really in the pit or hanging on the meat-hook, you don't have the energy to make contact. You watch people 'being normal', laughing, joshing, discussing minutiae or whatever and you simply can't join in. Because none of it makes sense. It's like they're talking a totally different language.

It's a hint of what you feel when someone you love has died – you're watching the world bustle by through thick dirty glass, swaddled in steel wool.

Yes, I could have tweeted. Yes, I could have put out a 'poor little me' yelp on Facebook. I could have written a 'hug me' blog. But, you know, I really didn't have the capacity. And then, as the days went by, I began to wonder. Does anyone even notice if you're not there? Bald answer? No.

I had to laugh really. I felt like the online equivalent of the old lady in the council flat, lying dead on the floor being eaten by her cats.

I guess it's a good lesson for the ego. Bottom line, if you're not out there shouting or wailing or emoting or waving your arms in the air, nobody notices. And, let's be honest, why should anyone? We've all got so many 'friends', so many followers and followees, how on earth can we keep tabs? Would I notice if one of my online 'friends' wasn't around for a week or so? Probably not. I'd assume they were busy or on holiday or just getting work done. One shouldn't take these things personally. Yet one does. Because when you're in the dark place, everything seems personal.

What am I saying here? A couple of things, I guess. Firstly, if you're heading down and can reach out, that's good – do it. But if you know you're someone who won't or can't, then seriously, I'd say move right away from the PC screen. Don't torture yourself.

Secondly, if you know people who are – shall we say – prone to fragility, then watch out for us. Not just for the messages we give out when we're online but for the times when we go dark, when we're off-line. Check in. Just a friendly nudge. It could be all we need to feel human again.

Don't let us lie on the kitchen floor being eaten by cats.

Like a cold wind, by Vivienne Tufnell

Like a cold wind on a summer's day
Raising a crop of goose-flesh;
Like a cloud across the sun's face
Turning the day into sudden twilight,
I feel the change inside me
And I wait to see if the cloud may pass.

Like the sudden silence before a storm,
The birds that cease to sing;
Like the eerie stillness of wild-life
Before the earth shakes and the sea flees,
I hear the roar of the angry waves
Rushing towards me to engulf the land.

Like the blank blink in the bully's eye
The second before he raises a fist;
Like the juddering engine before it stalls
Leaving you stranded at the lights,
It warns of worse to come
And teaches you how to duck.

When the fog comes floating in from the sea
It's time to sit down and wait
Turn on the lights, wrap up warm
Stay just where you are; do not fight.
For like fog, and darkness and the bully's wrath
This too, like all things, shall pass.

A footballer's despair: why we must stop singing 'Boys Don't Cry'

Tim Atkinson

Award-winning writer and blogger Tim Atkinson is a stay-at-home dad. It is a role he loves and which he combines with part-time teaching and, of course, his writing. His award-winning blog and online diary 'Bringing up Charlie' has a wide and loyal readership and his creative writing course has helped many people find their writing 'voice'. His own books include 'Writing Therapy' and 'Creative Writing - The Essential Guide'. Tim writes here of the suicide of a German professional footballer but, since it was first published, we have lost Wales manager Gary Speed and have seen a number of other high profile sportsmen come forward to admit that depression is an illness they have hidden for years. At last it seems the pressures on those at the top of their game are being acknowledged and by coming forward it is hoped that ALL men will feel better able to seek help.

On November 10th 2009, a man stepped onto the railway lines at the Neustadt-Eilvese crossing, on the route between Hamburg and Bremen in Germany. Two train drivers reported seeing him on the tracks but were unable to stop. Robert Enke was pronounced dead at the scene.

If the name seems familiar it might be because you read reports of the incident at the time. It was big news. Because although the suicide of a 36-year-old German male wouldn't normally receive world-wide press attention, Robert Enke was the German national goalkeeper, a highly paid professional footballer with a successful Bundesliga career and spells with Fenerbahce, Barcelona, Benfica and Borussia Mönchengladbach to his credit.

Although happily married, Enke and his wife were no strangers to tragedy. In 2006 their daughter Lara died at the age of two of a rare heart condition. And having been treated on and off for depression since 2003, Enke became increasingly worried that the couple's 18-month-old adopted daughter Leila would be taken into care if he went public about his depression. Nobody at his club, Hanover, had any idea about his problem.

Although he had been receiving treatment in private, on the day of his suicide Enke had cancelled all his appointments until further notice. In a note, the footballer apologised for the deliberate concealment but claimed that it had all been necessary in order to put his plan into action.

Necessary. It's a startling fact that although more women, on average, suffer mental illness (or should I say, seek treatment for it) male suicides far outnumber those of women. What is it about men like Enke (men like all of us) that means we can't express ourselves, even in the depths of despair? Why the need to cover up, self-medicate with alcohol or recreational drugs, deny and lie until it's too late?

Pretty soon after planning my novel *Writing Therapy* I knew that the first-person narrator of the story was going to have to be female. Although writing from the perspective of a teenage girl was likely to make the project far harder, there seemed no way a male narrator could credibly and candidly discuss his own depression and its treatment in the form of a confessional novel. It's not what 'we' do; we're men. We don't talk about our feelings; instead we either hit the bottle or bottle it all up. Until it's too late.

But it needn't be so. Boys need to talk too. And we – as parents – need to talk to them. And show them that it isn't always possible to be strong, to take what life throws at you, to go it alone. We all need help. And we need to make sure we're not too proud, stubborn or embarrassed to admit it.

Learning to love the rain again

Nettie Edwards

This is a moving description of living with Post Traumatic Stress Disorder by Nettie Edwards, a hugely talented artist, designer, iPhoneographer and iPhone collagist who creates work with her iPhone and iPad. I urge you to take a trip to her blog – www.lumilyon.blogspot.com – to see more of her work. It is simply striking in its intensity - eerie and disturbing; beautiful and mysterious.

A memory...

One of those sparkling early mornings that sometimes follow a night of heavy rain: birdsong rings brightly through air not yet choked with traffic fumes; the sun, low in slate-blue sky, glazes all with a golden wash. Inky shadows collect in the creases of the pavement. I usually miss all this: I'm rubbish at doing mornings.

You're getting hard on yourself again! Move on; bring your focus back to the present. What am I feeling right now? Absolutely nothing, I'm numb, there's no physical sensation, as if my life is happening in front of me on a cinema screen. This is heart-breaking; I used to love the rain. Then one day, the floods came and washed all the feeling away, leaving nothing but this feeling of not feeling.

But at least I managed to get out of bed this morning, managed to leave the house.

My mind wanders back a year...

I'm with my doctor, wrung out and desperate, telling her that I can't bear being inside my body any more. I'm a bag of nerves: physical tension, mood swings, irritability, anxiety, panic attacks, hyper-vigilance, and lack of concentration, memory and motivation. Exhausted from hardly sleeping, but having nightmares when I do, I'm afraid to step out of my house, most of all: of being with other people.

Then: words that I never wanted to hear myself saying: 'Do you think anti-depressants might be a good idea?' My doctor shakes her head. 'No, you're not presenting as a depressed person. To be honest, I don't know what's wrong with you or how I can help you...'

'Splish, splash, splosh! I like jumping in muddy puddles!' A child rushes past me on her way to school. Shock reverberates through my body: I'm dizzy, shaking and feel punched, convinced that I'm going to die. Post-

Traumatic Stress Disorder: you'll have heard it associated with war veterans, victims of violent crime or natural disasters. I have experienced none of these terrible things and yet here I am: my body so saturated with the chemicals of trauma that the unexpected appearance of a joyful child feels like an attack on my life. The wait for an assessment and diagnosis of this mental illness lasted many months, during which time my health deteriorated even further. Finally, due to the specific circumstances and complex nature of my trauma, I was asked: 'What kind of person would you like your therapist to be?' My response was 'A warm, creative, free-thinker who enjoys a good argument.' And so it was that Lucia came into my life...

Our room in the day centre that was once a Victorian-Gothic hospital is dim and sparsely furnished. I wonder out loud, how it is possible for anyone's mind to heal here. Lucia apologises: resources are tight and the Mental Health Services are moving out of the building soon. She's tried to cheer things up a bit with a few small posters. One features some Chinese calligraphy: Lucia explains that it reads 'Mindfulness' which is what I'm here to learn. The currently prescribed treatment for Post-traumatic Stress Disorder (PTSD) is Cognitive Behavioural Therapy (CBT), but Lucia has decided that Mindfulness will be a gentler path for me: 'Unlike many of my colleagues, I don't believe that I can transform you into some 'perfect' being, I just want to help you learn to be kind to yourself, accept yourself and what has happened to you. We're not going to talk about what brought you here because each time we do that, we allow those who have harmed you to harm you some more: let's not give them that power.' She slides a sheet of paper across the table and says gently, 'I'd like you do some homework'. There's a chart with questions: How do I describe myself? What are my core values? I'm flung into panic and begin to shake and weep, winding a tear-sodden and shredded paper tissue around and around my fingers. I don't know who I am. No! The truth is...I'm petrified to think or talk about who I am. Talking about me is part of how I got into this mess in the first place...

I'm in another room: this one's much more attractively decorated and comfortable, as seductive as the voice that coaxingly asks: 'How are you feeling today? It's ok, you're safe here, all feelings are welcome...' As I remember these words, the memories and rage tumble out, as they have done, over and over again...for how long? I don't know anymore, these memories have become my past, my present, my future. They've become part of my skin and bones.

Michele Rosenthal, a PTSD survivor who runs the support group www.healmyptsd.com has written: 'The bottom line is this - after a trauma occurs, survivors get lost in the gap between Before and After, Now and Then, Today and Yesterday, who they were pre-trauma and who they become as a result of experience. Nothing and no one is safe, stable, familiar, recognisable, known or dependable. Suddenly, the entire world has changed and how survivors perceived and knew themselves and their identities has shattered.'

If you have no sense of who you are, even the most simple of decisions becomes traumatic and can feel impossible to make: what shall I wear today? What do I want to eat? What shall I do? In my case, this led to complete shut-down, depression and self-loathing. I'm an artist and designer, I spent over 30 years of my life learning to trust my instincts to guide my creativity. PTSD robbed me of those instincts. It also robbed me of any vision of the future.

Mindfulness, a principal of Buddhist teaching, is the art of being in the present, of focusing thoughts on the here and now. Mastering Mindfulness takes great commitment and daily practice, but it doesn't matter if you do it for 30 seconds or 30 minutes, getting into the habit is what's important. There are many approaches, but the one that works best for me is Mindful Listening: wherever you are, close your eyes, and focus on the sounds around you. Make a mental note of each sound you hear. If you can, allow yourself to focus on them for a few minutes. You may find that your mind begins to calm down, your body to relax. The opportunity arises for you to gently nudge your thoughts from an anxious place to somewhere more calm and comfortable.

At the beginning of our work together, Lucia warned me that I would find it hard to let go of my pain and anxiety. She suggested I read Russ Ballard's book 'The Confidence Gap'. I'd like to suggest that you read it too. Ballard is a practitioner of Acceptance and Commitment Therapy (ACT) He writes: 'The goal of ACT is to create a rich and meaningful life, while accepting the pain that inevitably goes with it'

'What? You want me to accept what happened to me? You want me to forgive?' Now I'm angry, and I'm angry with myself for feeling angry....

Lucia pleads: 'Nettie, Nettie, show yourself some compassion, be kind to yourself.'

Slowly, the penny drops: I can't change what has happened to me but I can decide what's going to happen next...

Part of what happened next was that I learned to be less hard on myself for being ill. Self-compassion, in the form of accepting my limitations, didn't mean giving into them; it just made the baggage a little lighter for the journey. Lucia talked a lot about journeys: 'In your life, you are like a pioneer. It doesn't matter how many mountains you have to climb over, or rivers you have to swim across, you keep going west: because you have to!' She likened our work together as 'digging for the diamond inside that is 'Nettie''.

Anyone who has suffered with similar health issues will recognise the massive amounts of strength and courage it takes to recover. To begin with, it feels impossible: 'Look at the mess my life is in, how will I ever clear it all up?' Our negative thoughts and feelings have become so enmeshed with our identities, how is it possible to change them? Lucia and Russ suggest we don't even try but rather get on first-name terms. Now, whenever I begin to worry, I'll say to myself: 'Here we go, it's The Disaster Movie: I've seen this one before! BORING!' So I'm immediately distancing myself from anxious thoughts and can begin to think more effectively: 'Ok, I'm worried about the ferry to France sinking, that's not so daft, after all, there's a possibility that it might, but if I get myself so worked up before the trip that I'm rendered incapable of coping in an emergency, I'll be far less likely to survive'. In giving myself permission to have negative thoughts and feelings, some of their power diminishes. Furthermore, by placing them outside of myself, I'm able to see them for what they are: not an integral part of me, but separate and modifiable. Once I began to see my Mind's healing as a creative endeavour, I began to feel curious, and just a little excited...

Unless I choose to end it (and I have no intention of doing so) my life is going to carry on and I must continue trekking west through the uncharted landscape of recovery. It's up to me to choose the paths I'll follow and I must take responsibility for these choices. It's been almost a year now since Lucia and I first met. She had to work hard to earn my trust and it was a painful journey but by the end of our allotted time together, I was feeling much more in control of my depression and anxiety. Now I'm able to see glints of the 'diamond inside' that Lucia wanted me to uncover and polish. However, the loss of a loved-one was at the heart of my original trauma and as the PTSD symptoms diminish, what has begun to surface is the raw grief that was suppressed by them. My head may be clearer, but my heart will take longer to heal. For the last six months, I've been on the waiting list for NHS bereavement counselling.

Here and now...

I'm sitting in my garden. It's a beautiful autumn day: the sky is deep blue with fluffy clouds gathering and the sun feels hot on my cheeks despite a cool breeze. What can I hear? The last leaves rustle on the elder tree, wind chimes tinkle. Some way off: cars, an airplane, a dog barking. A tiny shiver runs down my spine and I notice that I'm smiling: it feels good to be alive. The tag on my teabags reads, 'You are, you have been, you will be, what you do' and this makes me notice all of the things that need doing in my garden: the things I've neglected because if my illness. Well, I'm not sure how much I'll get done today: I might get tired, I might not get myself mentally organised enough to complete one single task...but that's ok, I'm not going to beat myself up about it. I'm taking each moment as it comes and I'll welcome my difficult thoughts when they walk through the door, but I'm not going to invite them to sit down and have a cup of tea with me. After all, I now have other visitors to attend to. Today I'll throw a party for my small achievements, one of which is that slowly but surely, I'm learning to love the rain again.

Invisible, by Karla Smith

I am the invisible woman
Ignored by a room of people
Sat alone
Wondering why no one can see me
Always second best
Easy to push away
People think I'm weird
It's true I'm not like them
So I stay alone
I am the inferior woman
Fine when there's no one else
Ignored when someone better comes along
I am the one in a room of people
That no one particularly wants to know
I don't matter
It's ok to hurt my feelings
Because I am the invisible woman

And how did that make you feel?

Kit Johnson

Kit Johnson is a successful international businessman, who has had to battle through a diagnosis of bipolar disorder and wrestle with frequent moments of despair and suicidal thoughts, including two attempts. He is brutally honest and thoroughly non -PC (be warned!) about the help he sought though tried and tested channels, as he took medication and various therapies - all to no avail. He says that he discovered humour and home-spun philosophies could save him from the worst excesses of his condition. Learn more about Kit Johnson and his book 'Dodging Suicide – A Lifetime's Preoccupation' through Amazon.com, or at www.dodgingsuicide.com.

A few years ago I went to see a psychiatrist and said 'Could you help me out?' and he said, 'Sure which way did you come in? ' So that's that profession dealt with....

What about meds? I once presented my wife with some Olympic condoms; gold, silver, and bronze, and asked her to choose. She said 'Let's go for silver and see if you can come second for a change!' As male readers may concur, SSRI's have the exact opposite effect. So that's meds dealt with....

I went to my GP and asked him what he thought about Cyclothymics and he said 'Well I couldn't eat a whole one.' So that's the doctor dealt with......

Ok, ok, ok time to inject some sanity – sorry no pun intended. I am not against any of the above, but after 45 years with bipolar, I worked out nothing was working for me. The rule has to be: 'whatever does it for you', go with it.

I do think we, as a society, look for silver bullet solutions too readily; and frankly they don't exist. I do not believe I can be cured, but I can manage it. The very action of seeking help made me feel a failure. Taking the pills to control my brain made me feel a freak. And you know what – I AM NOT! After all, I might already have made you laugh – yes?

My epiphany came the day I realised mocking my condition, using the gifts of humour I'd been given, suddenly made me feel good – proud even. And I've practised it ever since. And when my self-deprecation fails me, I hit YouTube and watch some of my favourite comedians. And I do feel better. Of course it won't do it for everyone, not even me on occasion, but I commend it as something else to consider as you seek that Holy Grail.

48

I discovered I was bipolar in my teens. If you liken life to a rodeo, it felt like someone had seen fit to knobble me with haemorrhoids. I spent a good deal of my life feeling angry, so I was vulnerable to trying anything and in my experience, that can lead to a succession of disappointments, especially when you realise you are still the same. But at the time if someone had told me that probing sheep's entrails whilst playing 'will ye no come back again' on bagpipes, sitting on a camel would do it – I'd have tried it.

A friend of mine went to his doctor and said, 'I wake up every morning and start singing Delilah'. The doctor says he had Tom Jones' disease. 'Is it common?' asked my friend. 'Well it's not unusual......'

Bipolar is unusual. But it need not cripple you. Like its close stable-mate, depression, it is debilitating, but that's no reason to feel shame or pretend you don't have it and suffer in silence. I now count my blessings. After all, if I did not have the condition I wouldn't be here writing this, and hopefully bringing a bit of joy to people.

So you've just had a measured dose of Kit Johnson, and in those immortal and largely useless words uttered by your counsellor, 'How did that make you feel?' A little bit better I hope.

How does depression look to you?

Emma Major

Emma Major is a full-time mum, part-time volunteer, part-time career advisor and a licensed lay minister. She talks of her lifelong issues with depression and post-natal depression and her words will, I am sure, strike a chord with many. She writes with a visual, creative energy that takes us on a journey through a life of depressive experiences. She has her own blogs at www.llmcalling.blogspot.com and www.majorloveoffilm.blogspot.com

I agreed to write about my experience of depression, but being faced with an empty screen was daunting and left me wondering where to start. Then I realised that when I thought about my depression I saw images, so here goes.

How does depression look to you?

Is it far away, something that happens to others, just a shadow in the background?

Is it black and all-encompassing and around you every day?

Is it blinding white?

Or panic red?

For me depression has looked different each time I have been struck by it; I guess that's why I never spot the very early stages, although I'm getting better. I have gone through my life and its ups and downs with the aid of images, and questions.

Childhood: Why? What's going on? How can I be popular at school?

Only now, looking back, do I realise how badly bullied I was at school. How I hated playtimes and PE lessons and the endless party invitations I never received. Everyday my self-esteem plummeted and I thought less of myself. In the end I believed myself to be worthless and useless.

I have been battling against that ever since. It comes back with a vengeance when I am in a depressive episode; it eats away at my soul and grows and grows so that I believe it all over again.

Teenage: What's happening to me? Why doesn't anyone like me? Is this what everyone's life is like?

Secondary school was, if anything, worse than primary school. OK the lessons were better and the fact that we were streamed helped, and the way I was with different people. But somehow the bullying followed me and then was taken up by others. Weirdly though, I found a way to cope; I learnt that if I ignored the taunts and stayed friendly they gave up a bit. In the end I was providing homework help to those kids who had the vicious tongues. It would be fine in a small group, but in a class or larger group I was the victim.

Late teens: Why am I not enough? Will anyone ever love me? How will I go on from here? How can I take all this pain away?

At 16 things changed; I found myself somehow and joined a group that felt right and gave me the confidence to be me. I even got a boyfriend and life was amazing, best ever, for over a year.

And then it was over and my first massive depression came upon me. I couldn't function, couldn't see anything but the end, and I tried to bring it about. If I couldn't keep that love then I was unlovable. There was no point. It took me a couple of years to really come out of this episode, a move away to university and my first real girl friends; finally I started to realise my worth.

Early twenties: When is the next holiday? When can we escape again? Why isn't my career making me happy?

I met my husband at university; we found jobs close to each other, we moved across the country together and we bought our first flat. We were engaged and planning a wedding and we were succeeding in our careers. Life was good. Yet depression struck again. More subtle this time, I started realising that I was living for the holidays, the times when we could escape real life and be just us. It was escapism I was craving and eventually I couldn't get enough. This time a promotion and job move was the cure.

Late 20s: Is it morning? Why am I so exhausted? Do I have to get out of bed today?

This is how depression felt in my late 20s. A void.

An expanse of unexplored, unknown and unforgiving land surrounding my dark hole.

Yet I was happily married, with a successful career and none of it made any sense.

I could barely get out of bed. I was diagnosed with Chronic Fatigue Syndrome, but looking back it was clearly the good old depression. And something in me realised it because this was when I finally made it into counselling, a decision for which I will be eternally grateful to myself.

Miscarriages: Why me? Why my babies? Will I ever be a mother? Do I deserve to ever be a mum?

Anyone would be depressed when they suffer grief; well that is what miscarriage is. Have three in just over a year, with fertility treatments in between, and it is completely understandable why I was as depressed as I was. After my third miscarriage I could barely function at all; sometimes I got out of bed, occasionally I left the house. I avoided my friends, my GP, my counsellor. I just didn't want to feel better. And then I fell pregnant again, and this time I stayed pregnant, and then my baby was born.

Post Natal Depression: Panic, panic, panic. What if something happens to her? Will I ever be a good enough mother?

I had my much longed for, much loved, much adored baby. I could not have been happier. OK I was stressed about everything, but that's normal for first time mums. OK I couldn't leave her side or let anyone else do anything, but then she was my baby that we had waited five years for. OK I had no idea what to do with myself when she was asleep, but surely that was sleep deprivation?

It took over four months to be diagnosed with Post Natal Depression (PND); mainly because I was atypical. I was happy and contented and functioning; but I was panicky and anxious and terrified something would happen to my girl. I didn't want time away, not at all; I wanted never to leave her side. I wanted to always gaze into her beautiful eyes and hold her soft fingers. But luckily my GP saw what was happening and was kind and gentle and took me through the fact that I was anxious because I was grieving the loss of my previous babies. Yes I was depressed, but it was OK and acceptable and treatable.

I had tried anti-depressants previously in my life and hated them, hated them! The numbness and the sloppiness and the lack of joy; but these ones were different apparently. And different they were, they didn't take away the joy, but they eased the anxiety, and within two months I was feeling much more like me again.

And now: Why am I isolating? Why am I sleeping so much? Where has all my positivity gone?

This is how my depression feels now.

If my normal emotional state is a rainbow in a blue sky, then my depressed times feel like a faded rainbow in a stormy sky. I am still on my medication, but only a low dose with slight increases for periods if needed. I see my counsellor come what may, even when I know it'll be hard. And I share how I felt and how I feel – it helps.

Life is good, it is real, it has its ups and downs like anyone else has.

But.......

Now I don't panic.

Now I see the signs, even if a little later than I'd like.

Now I go to see my GP to adjust my meds.

Now I increase the frequency of my counselling sessions.

Now I reach out to friends and family and stop isolating myself.

For today my depression is a condition I live with, like diabetics live with their condition. Like them I regularly check how I'm doing, and I adjust my therapies accordingly. I might one day be free of this thing called depression; but for now I live with it, openly, acceptingly and hopefully.

Now every day is a rainbow; it just varies in its brightness.

Life Force, by Suzie Grogan

The day is grey, a spiky mizzle and a chilly wind
Catch my breath as I walk slowly to the lake.
Sharp stones crunch down beneath me
As the rowing boat drifts gently from the shore.

Sky endless drab; but all seems green or shades of
Blue perhaps, or slate grey flecked with purple heather.
Small sandy landslips scar the distant slopes,
Far paths snake up fell sides, a patchwork of enclosures bounded by stone
walls.

Swifts overhead, batlike, diving like spitfires to skim the surface of the
water
Catching darting midges.
My boat cuts slowly through the small waves with a gentle dip
and water ahead like electricity shivers silver across the lake.

Reeling away, a circuit is too far, my aching limbs feel drained
But there it is: unfettered Force, violent physicality
Relentless in its spumy violence strikes
Down the purple slopes, a patchwork rent with startling ease.

This place; resistance futile, water outburst, shifting rock and soil
Suits my mood, the flowing water tipping to the surface,
My reflection, interrupted, shivers
And all the world flows from my eyes, set free by Force and Fell.

S.I.S.N.M (Suffer In Silence No More) - How supporting others can save us all

Nic Elgey

Nic Elgey is manager and founder of S.I.S.N.M (Suffer In Silence No More), a peer support online group for mental health sufferers. It was always Nic's dream to help others and create something that would make a difference. Here she tells us the story of how all of this unfolded.

My name is Nic Elgey and I am a part time retail sales assistant, but I am also manager and founder of S.I.S.N.M (Suffer In Silence No More) an online peer support group for mental health sufferers.

Born on March 18th 1981 I live at home with my wonderful mum and dad in Nottinghamshire. I have lived here for the whole 31 years of my life. Some may say still living at home at my age is strange, but they don't understand my illness makes it this way. To keep me safe if I feel down, feel like I want to cut myself (because sometimes I really do). There is always someone there to stop it from happening, to talk me round. I also have a sister I am very close to and a best friend, Kristine Long, who is my absolute rock!

My life was quite a normal one. I had a lovely childhood, the best my mum and dad could give me. My big issue was school - I hated it from beginning to end. I was never a popular girl, did not have many friends and was quiet. I suppose that was the start of me becoming a bit of a recluse, because I wasn't interested. I was quite happy on my own doing my own thing. I was, however, confident around the people I trusted - my friends and family. I was happy and I did go out occasionally, but this all changed and my life got turned upside down in 1996. I lost a friend - he died in a road traffic accident. I remember it well. Just before Christmas on a foggy night, as he crossed the main road, he didn't see the car coming towards him and the car did not see him. It happened close to my house too, so when I went out I was reminded everywhere. I had never had a big loss before and it overwhelmed me.

I actually got to a point where I thought I was going insane. I couldn't understand what was happening. The things I used to be able to do I couldn't any more. Going out was a huge chore. I'd be panicky, feel dizzy, faint, shaky - the usual symptoms of anxiety, but I had no idea what it was, so I found myself crying in public and unable to face the world. At my worst I locked myself in the bathroom and refused to come out until mum agreed I did not have to go to school the next day. For three months I never went anywhere. Instead of crying in public, I did it at home instead or just stayed in bed. With the help of a good doctor, medication and a nurse who came round to take me out, I gradually got my life back. At the start it was just a walk up the drive, then the end of the road until I made it into town. It was hard; there were days I wanted to give up and at my worst I used to be physically sick before going out (so much so I hardly ate anything as it made me feel sick) because of the total fear of it. Some mornings I fought and fought not to be sick, because the ritual of throwing up every morning was not healthy. I did see three different therapists and got rid of all three also! Not because they were incapable, I just found therapy was useless to me. I sat there while they tried to tell me what was going on and I thought 'How do they know?' I didn't trust them. I trust few in life - that way I don't get hurt. Surely these people read it and study from books? I actually am going through it. I felt patronised, so I just didn't bother to go.

I felt trapped and alone like I needed somewhere to turn where people understood me, but there was nowhere. That was when I thought, if this kind of network does not exist then why don't I do something about it? This would be the thing that would make a difference and a cause very close to my heart. I knew what it was like to feel alone, desperate and unhappy. How many more out there were feeling the same? This was my turning point to get better, so I somehow got the strength to be brave and become strong.

S.I.S.N.M was born on 4th April 2011. I created a page on Facebook in the hope I would get 50 members if I was lucky. No way could I ever have predicted what happened next! It seems my hunch was right; by October 2011 I had 500+ people coming to use my page, saying that I had saved their life, people felt like they belonged and how some had been alone for a long, long time. This made me feel both touched and happy that I had achieved what I had set out to do.

Since then the group has gone from strength to strength. I even have a celebrity patron, Julie Etchingham, who reads ITV news at 10 in the UK. I asked her, because it is a cause also close to her and was delighted when she said yes. She has given us nothing but 100% support and we are so very lucky.

More than that though, I see people making friends with each other, opening up and supporting and that is down to me. From one idea that just grew in to something massive.

I am very proud of what I have done and now have high hopes that we will continue to be a success. I have my own team of staff who are brilliant. On March 18th the group will reach a new milestone. I will be launching the group's official website for people to come, read about us, and find useful links, blogs and information on different things. Hopefully people will come and join us. There are so many people still to reach out to and I will do my best to reach them all. I also hope to become a registered charity and do drop-in centres, and go round schools etc. and give talks on mental health, so it is better understood. Then maybe people won't judge or pick fun about something we can't help. There needs to be a new look on mental health to rid the stigma and let people know we are just the same as them no matter what we suffer. We all have baggage right?

I am so thankful for all of this and to all involved too. Creating this has helped me feel better and I really feel genuinely happy and content for the first time in years. My message to everyone is don't give up you can do it! I am proof that dreams really can come true.

My own biggest critic

Louise Berry

Louise is an Assistant Mental Health Recovery Worker working with people with severe mental illness and has also been a volunteer on the telephone helpline 'Mindline', dealing with callers who are experiencing mental distress or caring for someone with mental distress, for more than three years. She has, however, had her own battles with depression, anxiety and low self-esteem for much of her life and describes here how she is coming to terms with these aspects of her personality.

For most of my life I have experienced anxiety and depression. Why is this? I trace the beginning of my major battle with depression and anxiety to adolescence. I was very shy at school, not least as a result of being bullied. This set me apart and contributed towards my negative feelings towards myself. I struggled with dealing with my feelings; back then I didn't label it depression. I eventually even set myself apart from my own family by spending all my time at home in my room. This turned into a little more than the usual teenage angst.

I do not know if my problems with depression and anxiety would have been just as bad had I not been bullied at school. I do not know if life would have been any easier if my circumstances had been different. I didn't have an abusive upbringing.

I do though now have a life-long, clinical depression that never really goes away.

The world can seem like a very empty and bleak place when I am at my lowest. A full-blown depressive period is like having a heavy mass around you that crushes your ability to function even on a fairly basic level. Everyday tasks can seem like climbing a very steep hill, every step is a huge effort. This results in a desire to just hide away and avoid doing as much as possible. Avoidance can result in self-directed anger and frustration. I constantly question myself. Why can't I just get on with my day like everyone else? Why am I so useless? Sometimes I also feel guilty for being self-indulgent; surely there are people worse off than me?

Depression is a dark, oppressive, deflating and even frightening feeling that makes me feel isolated even in the company of others. I feel completely lacking in self-worth and have a desire to crawl into a deep hole and remain there until the feeling passes. I tend to feel extremely self-conscious and 'exposed' when not on my own. A depressive period can last for days or weeks, even months.

My anxiety can have a definite cause or come on unexpectedly. I think people who don't experience extreme anxiety can't realise how debilitating it can be. It can completely dominate your life and restrict it to an enormous degree. At my worst, around nine years ago, I became almost agoraphobic and it took me several years to feel brave enough to begin facing the world again. I would be convinced that people could see that there was something wrong and I had a real fear of being stared at, judged and thought to be 'mad' and this kept me at home.

When I am feeling at my lowest, every task takes the maximum amount of effort. When I am at my most anxious, I am constantly checking that everything I do is correct, over and over again and wearing myself out mentally in the process. With anxiety and depression one feeds off the other – the anxiety makes me feel that nothing I ever do will be good enough and the depression makes me want to give up – what's the point when I will never get it right?

I have been diagnosed with depression, Obsessive Compulsive Disorder and Generalised Anxiety Disorder – which in a nutshell means that I worry about anything and everything, regardless of whether the threat is real or imagined. If I have something specific to worry about, a relatively minor problem can appear to reach catastrophic proportions. No matter how hard I try, rationalisation doesn't really work. Part of the problem is the sub-conscious fear that if I stop worrying then something bad will happen. Ultimately, of course, I know that worrying for the sake of worrying doesn't solve anything. I try to rationalise my fear and relax but this is often impossible.

I carry an assumption that other people are stronger than I am, handle situations better than I do and are generally more competent at coping with life. They are more able than me, are more likable, better company and generally have more to offer. I constantly compare myself to others, unfavourably. This has made me go to great lengths to try to impress people; to go that extra mile just to try to 'keep up' with everybody else, and then hate myself for being so needy. I never meet my own exacting standards and always let myself down.

I have accessed the health service through my GP to help me to deal with my problems. Although I have a very good doctor, I am now trying to carry on without any help. I have tried anti-depressants and found them to be of some use when I have felt particularly badly affected but ultimately I know that I need to help myself. A part of me thinks 'it's only anxiety and depression – it's not like I have a severe mental illness'. The trouble is, as anyone who experiences long term, clinical depression knows, there is nothing 'only' about it when you are in the midst of it. It is exhausting, can appear to be never ending and dominates every experience. It affects close relationships, making the sufferer angry, defensive and fearful.

I think my greatest desire is to be able to live more in the moment - not waste so much time and energy thinking about what will happen tomorrow, next week or on some other future date, or to 'catastrophise' what to most people would be minor problems. The trouble is, I have lived with anxiety for so long that it takes a long time to retrain the brain to appreciate the here and now and not worry about the future. It is my default position. Complete self-acceptance would be a very significant achievement for me. A course of Cognitive Behavioural Therapy has been very helpful but it's not a 'cure' and wasn't really long enough. I have a lot of on-going work to do and it is a constant process. Knowing yourself and helping yourself can be two very different things.

I am also an over-the-top 'people pleaser', with a desperate desire to meet with the approval of other people. I have to admit that I am far too sensitive to criticism from other people, even at times when given positively, with good intent.

Ultimately, I am my own biggest critic. Maybe one day I will even meet with my own approval.

One year on – a new life

Mark K.

Writing has long been a release for Mark K during bouts of deep depression. It has only been recently that, after changes to his diagnosis and treatment, he has started writing when not under the cloud of depression. He is using this new-found freedom to write on mental health issues, to help raise awareness of problems faced by sufferers & to fight the stigma associated with mental illness. Mark has also kindly allowed me to reproduce one of his poems in this anthology - 'Loneliness'.

Just 12 months ago I was diagnosed as bipolar. I was told I suffered from social phobia and PTSD, had anxiety issues and was mildly obsessive-compulsive. Yet the year that has just passed is the best I've had in probably 15 years or more. How can it be that despite this alarming list of mental illnesses, I'm so much better today than I was?

The answer is quite simple. Before this diagnosis I was being treated based on an 11-year-old diagnosis, a diagnosis I had believed was incorrect for most of that time. In early 2000 I was diagnosed with major depression – a label that I would live with for the next 11 years. I never realised it at the time, but once you're labelled by a doctor as having a certain illness, it can be very, very hard to get it changed, even if you know it's incorrect.

Having the diagnosis allowed me to do my own research on the subject and it wasn't too long before I realised that I didn't have just depression, I was probably bipolar instead. But getting this across to those treating me didn't seem to work. I can't blame them really; my periods of depression were very long, months at a time, compared to a week or so of highs every now and then. So when I saw them I was always down and probably didn't get the details across fully.

So I lived the label. Many different treatments and medications were tried, none that ever seemed to get me 'right'. Some worked to a degree, allowing me a little freedom to actually get out of the house occasionally. But generally, things stagnated. The long periods of darkness were still there, as were the uncontrollable mood swings and rages. Sadly, it was my family who suffered most during this period and in the end it was too much and the family broke up. I became a virtual hermit.

Finally I had enough of city living – too many people, too much noise. I just couldn't take it anymore. So a few years ago I moved back to the area I was born, a large country town. Things didn't change much. I still didn't go out unless I had to and my new GP kept up the treatments for major depression. I had the label and that's what I was – majorly depressed.

Towards the end of 2010 I started doing things out of character even for me. I became obsessed with something and just couldn't let it go, no matter how I tried. I kept doing what I was doing, saying to myself the whole time that it had to stop, it was going too far. But I couldn't stop and eventually things got out of hand. My world collapsed around me again. What I had been doing hurt people around me badly, people I truly cared about. It was too much for me. I had to do something to change what was happening to me.

I booked an extra-long session with my GP; I was going to tell him everything I could, make him understand I was not just depressed. So I talked and talked. I told him everything, even things that I had been too ashamed to tell anyone – how bad the lows were, thoughts of death and suicide, feeling I was a waste of time and space. How the highs were too high; days without sleep, mind going a million miles an hour, unable to sit still, spending all my money and more without a care in the world. How I seemed to get something started and become obsessed with it, no matter how bad things got I just had to keep going.

And he listened, he really listened. He agreed that I was bipolar, but then shocked me by adding a few more things. The anxiety I understood. I would go shopping and within a couple of minutes I would be sweating and shaking. Anytime I went out the thought was always how quickly I could get home. I never realised that my not wanting to go anywhere was more than just the depression – on the few occasions I did go out to things like a relatives birthday, I would always hide in a dark corner, just staying long enough to be polite. And no matter how far away I was, I would still drive straight home as soon as I left. I never felt safe until I was back in my own place.

The big surprise for me was being labelled mildly OCD. Me? Isn't OCD those people who wash their hands every five minutes, or have to have everything arranged exactly so? Apparently not, there appears to be a lot of different ways to display OCD. My GP pointed out a number of areas in my past where I had behaved in ways that indicated OCD. This included what I did that led to me coming to see him this time. For me, the OCD is not being able to let something go, no matter what. I get something in my head and will just keep at it until it's done or it blows up in my face.

But at least the bad way I had been in for the previous few months had one good outcome – I finally got what appears to have been a full and correct diagnosis. Which means my treatment was changed there and then. My new medications included anti-psychotics for the first time. And sessions with a new counsellor, who now has the correct diagnosis, meaning what we talk about is relevant to my current situation. All of which seem to be helping.

And this is why the last year has been so much better than the past. I can now go out more, even socialise. I've even taken up ten-pin bowling several times a week – though that almost became another costly obsession. One of my brothers recently commented on how different I am now. He had stopped visiting me because he just didn't know what to say to me, I was so unresponsive. But now he feels like I'm at least in the same country.

I am starting to recognise when a period of depression or mania is starting, something I've never been able to do. And, for the last few months at least, the highs and lows haven't been to the extremes that they once were. I am much more social when I go out - I actually talk to people. I don't know how but I've even managed to get a wonderful woman in my life who is helping me more than she could ever know. She gets me thinking, challenging labels placed on me by others and myself.

My life is still far removed from what many would consider 'normal', but it has been much better than the one I lived since being diagnosed with depression 12 years ago. Things aren't perfect, they never can be. But at least I have the strength and will to face each day as it comes. It took a major upheaval in my life to again stand up and says, 'Hey, things aren't right. I need more help.' But it was enough to get me on the road to looking at myself differently and coming to terms with my condition. I think it was the first time I really accepted me, accepted that I had an illness and needed to do what needs to be done to get some control over it.

There are still periods in which I struggle, and getting out of bed some mornings is still a great effort. But things are better, and most days I can face the world. Well, some of it anyway. I've gone from thinking I deserve nothing in this life to realising everyone is entitled to a little happiness. And I'm grabbing mine with both hands and not letting go.

Autophobia or How I Stop Worrying and Learn to Love my Ego

Debra (surname held back for personal reasons)

Debra has had a black dog nipping at her heels since early adolescence and whilst she has managed to tame it for the most part, it still insists on coming out to play when least expected. Anxiety-filled moments could range from worrying about the morning alarm-clock not going off to believing that she will almost certainly die before she's had a chance to pen all of her writing projects. She says that researching her family history and being a mother to an energetic daughter have gained her some shred of sanity in a world filled with crazy dogs and dark veiled shadows. You can read her family history blog at www.pocketfulloffamilymemories.blogspot.com

To say that I suffer from depression sounds alien to me. The dictionary defines suffering thus:

To feel pain or distress

To tolerate or endure pain, evil, injury or death

To appear at a disadvantage

What I find interesting about the first two definitions is that suffering sounds like it could be a good thing. It's normal and okay to suffer, to feel, to tolerate or endure. However, my past experience with suffering was definitely the third definition. I didn't know any other definition until much later in life.

To my mind, suffering implied that I may not ever recover, that I was destined to be at a disadvantage forever.

A popular Australian 70s band sang, 'Ego is not a dirty word'. This couldn't be further from the truth when it came to my upbringing. I was fed on a daily diet of humility and modesty from birth, where depression was a very dirty word. Depression ran rife in my extended family and yet, before I sought help, nobody discussed it or dealt with it. It was swept under the carpet alongside the failed marriages, frequent job or house changes, and ill health, including the interminable 'c' word (whisper it with me now: cancer).

When did my depression start? From very early on in my life, I now believe. I had a fairly unremarkable childhood; divorced parents, moving frequently, crippling shyness intermingled with a deep-seated need to please everybody (anxiety). An only child brought up by a single mother. But then came some pretty nasty shocks that no child should have to endure, which led me to a tumultuous adolescence and a manic introduction to adulthood.

My father had married again (starting a new family), followed by my move from England to Australia with my mother. I constantly felt torn between two countries, two parents, and two lives. The move threw me into utter chaos and, dare I admit it, desolation. Getting through school in a new country - pimples, periods, boys, exams, graduating, getting a job, more boys - was a nightmare ride. I didn't have a clue who I was, which only led to more anxiety and depression.

How did I deal with my depression? In my teens and early 20s, I didn't. I was an ostrich who continually put her head in the sand. My only salvation was music. It became my lifeline. I listened to music all day, every day. I danced and I sang, and I mimed and I dreamed. For more than 20 years of my life, music was my only currency. I dabbled with boys and alcohol, like most girls my age, but only music truly inspired me. When I turned 27 I found out, through professional counselling, that there was so much more in life to discover.

Telling my family that I was going to seek counselling was one of the hardest things I have ever done. Largely, I received confused stares, uncomfortable silences and very little in the way of support. Nobody knew what to say to me.

By 1992 I was desperate for answers. Why do I feel so miserable all the time? Why am I not happy? What is wrong with me? What have I done to cause this? By definition I had it all; a husband, a successful nursing career, a new home. I had no reason to be sad, right?

You might be thinking, 'But you live in Australia, with sandy beaches and unending sunshine, I wouldn't be miserable with that every day.' This is a myth, but I have lost count of how many times I have had this said to me. No matter what I tell them, they think I'm 'off my head'. What they don't understand is that depression is not purely environmental. Depression is a condition, and it can strike anybody at any time regardless of where in the world you live.

I couldn't have picked a better professional counsellor to meet with. She was one of the most humble yet self-assured women I have ever known and to this day I still smile when I think of her. I remember the day when she looked across the room at me and asked, 'Do you love your mum?' 'Yes' came my automatic response. 'Do you like your mum?' Silence. Why wouldn't my mouth move? Of course I should say I like her. She's my mum! I had no idea that being asked this question 20 years ago would spark a major journey of self-discovery (which I am still on). That question slowly picked away at and unravelled the powerful issue of depression in my family. In me.

I would like to sound all 'new-age' and say I embraced my depression but that implies that depression is an all-knowing, all-loving thing. I prefer to say that I am making friends with it. Like a friend, there are moments when it is there for me and I am glad and even comforted by the knowledge that at least I feel something. Then again, there are moments when I just want to be left alone. With a stubborn determination, I turn my back on it and ignore it until it goes away. This second option never works though. It just waits for me to turn back around and then it smacks me on the head even harder than the first time.

I have had to learn how to pay attention to my moods. This is not easy, especially when, for most of your life, you have been discouraged from thinking only about yourself. Remember, I was brought up on heavy doses of humility. The art of listening to my self-talk every day, with all its highs and lows, ebbs and flows, was repugnant. It took some convincing on my part to wade through the negativity and get to the core issues. I had to check and re-check myself constantly, and notice when my depressive state first showed signs of rearing its ugly head.

Recognising the signs can still be exhausting. I have to factor in things such as pre-menstrual syndrome and take into account that external things can affect my moods. More importantly though, I have had to learn to turn off those self-deprecating 'tapes' in my head that told me I was not good enough.

Nowadays, I get through my 'bouts' of depression with genealogy, family history, and writing. I also draw strength from being a mother (when I'm not fretting about being the world's worst!). I like to think that I have achieved a greater level of understanding through researching my ancestral past, finding a place in the world, knowing where I have come from and where I fit in to the ever-growing tapestry of life. I am passionate about my life history. I am also passionate about my spirituality. Without getting in touch with my inner strengths and weaknesses, and understanding that one cannot exist without the other, I am destined to be forever soulless. Being grateful for the ebbs and flows in my daily life is yet another work in progress.

Depression sours like vinegar, but 'I'm Fine'.....

Chris Rugg

Chris Rugg is an award-winning mental health advocate and is keen to raise awareness of the subject through his poetry. Elsewhere in this book you can find 'I'm Fine', his own personal favourite, and 'The Law of Sod'. Chris is one of those people who always puts others before himself, however poorly he feels. I count myself fortunate to be his friend and take this opportunity to thank him for his incredible support.

Clinical depression is the malignant all-pervading vinegar that sours mind, body and soul. It knows no barriers and does not distinguish between race, creed, colour, class, sex or sexuality. Therefore, no matter what they may think, no one is immune from this, or any other form of mental distress.

Those looking in ask, 'What's wrong?' Unless they are here or have been here, I cannot explain. It is not like a sore throat for which you suck a lozenge, or a broken bone, which you repair with a plaster cast; I wish it were that simple. Unfortunately, there are no lozenges or plaster casts for the mind, though there are anti-depressants. Without them, I would be considerably worse or dead!

To lie in bed at night with every bone, muscle and sinew aching for sleep, with a mind which is fully awake and racing with thoughts that do not allow sleep is, at times, almost insufferable. Hamlet in his soliloquy 'To be or not to be' says, 'To sleep: perchance to dream'. A better version would be 'To sleep: perchance to rest'. Real sleep is nothing but an elusive daydream; if it were not dark at night I would know every inch of my ceiling and every cobweb and spider that lurks there. The nearest I get to sleeping is the short period of deep uneasy 'sleep' towards the end of the night, from which I wake exhausted.

Moods swing from high to low, low to high within hours with no apparent reason; it is as though mood is a separate being in total control of one's mind and essence. The highs do not last very long, perhaps five or six hours at most, whereas the lows can last anything from a few hours to several weeks. Over the years, I have developed ways and means to hide or mask my moods from friends, relatives and work colleagues.

Clinical depression is not only about mood swings it also creates or heightens the following:

Fear of losing friends

This is a very real, continuing, and probably selfish fear of losing my close friends by saying or doing something to offend or upset them. These friends give me support and invaluable friendship. I hope I support them and return their friendship. The support they give is support that a family never can give because we have had, and are sharing experiences, which a family cannot imagine.

Fear of letting people down, not being good enough

Although linked to the fear of losing friends this fear has a much wider significance in that it applies to virtually everything said or done. It is a constant striving for perfectionism, which is unachievable and therefore leads to feelings of dissatisfaction, frustration and under-achievement.

Fear of the next episode

This may sound dramatic to those who have no experience of clinical depression. It is not so much a fear of the depression, although that is frightening enough; it is the fear of what will be contemplated or done to escape the desperation which comes with the depression.

Isolation

Brought about by the desire to run, to escape from everything, to find total peace and quiet and to be completely alone. Finding isolation seems to help the recovery process, albeit a temporary recovery. There is often a desire to just curl up in a corner, hide and never come out.

Confusion and lack of concentration

Racing and erratic thoughts do not allow the mind to process incoming information immediately. It becomes a large tangle of thoughts and I can then give the impression of not listening or paying attention. This is not the case; the information is taken in and eventually processed and an answer or opinion, if required, given later. The same racing thoughts can make it difficult to concentrate and easy to become distracted, particularly by sounds or movement.

Poor memory

A perplexing phenomenon, where events, conversations and even school lessons from 40 or 50 years ago are remembered as if they happened yesterday, yet it is impossible to remember something from just one minute ago.

Low or no self-esteem

Feelings of worthlessness, shame and guilt brought on by the inability to interact at an acceptable everyday level, loss of energy and willpower, feeling incapable of simple everyday tasks, so that something like changing the bed becomes comparable with climbing Mount Everest.

'Nermality'

Those on the outside have a false impression that depression is just feeling low; they are so wrong. Of course I am not always high or low. Usually I am somewhere in between, what I call 'nermal' (nearly normal). In this state of 'nermality', I may be experiencing highs or lows, but I am better able to manage my life and mind. 'Nermality' can be a very fragile and vulnerable state to be in, where it is easy for a trigger to send the mind tumbling back into depression.

Discrimination

One of the most powerful triggers is encountering stigma, prejudice, discrimination; call it what you will. Discrimination, especially verbal, is one of those things which you cannot dodge, cannot see coming, and it is directed right at you. It instigates anger, low self-esteem, and avoidance, the fear of not being good enough, confusion and lack of concentration, and the need for isolation. This leads to low morale, which can - and very often does - lead to another episode of depression. Discrimination in the workplace is widespread and many managers seem to have little or no control over it, often because they do not see it or choose to ignore it.

Clinical depression is treatable and manageable; it just takes a lot of time, patience, hard work and willpower (because of the nature of the beast, willpower is the most elusive) to get there. Nevertheless, please be assured that it can be done!

I'm Fine

Chris Rugg

Hello Chris, you're looking well, I thought you were ill!

Look into my eyes; see the countless private tears they have wept

See the overwhelming weariness, which makes my body ache

See the sleepless nights too many to remember

See the turmoil and pain which is my mind

Feel the moods so dark, so powerful they have substance

Feel the weight of thoughts so heavy they cannot move

Feel the blameless guilt and shame so undeniable

I want to shout SORRY!! For what I don't know

All of these hidden behind a thin veneer

A veneer of false happiness and well-being

These and so much more

Just the tip of the iceberg that is Depression

Should I say? No, I'd better not.

Thank you, yes, I'm fine, how are you?

What depression feels like ~ a moment by moment analysis

Vivienne Tufnell

I'm sinking. I must have been sinking for ages but I couldn't see it. I try to speak but words won't come. They feel stale, overused and meaningless as I turn them over in my head like worn-out clothes. I fall silent, all the things I might once have talked of now long forgotten, like those far off days on a summer afternoon after school, that lose meaning when you try and put those memories into some sort of adult order. My mind stutters, the words dry; there seems no point in speaking them. It won't mean anything to anyone who wasn't there at the time, and the memories vanish in a swirl of numbness.

I am eyes, seeing and observing, a pair of eyes in an ocean of nothingness. Some things are too bright, as if illuminated from within by the heat of decay; other things are dull as if a coating of filmy dirt covers them. I know something is beautiful but I feel nothing. It doesn't touch me.

I am ears, hearing and remembering, but for what purpose I do not know. Like an idiot, I listen, trying to catch words in the chatter of sparrows, and make sense of the wind in the trees.

Someone once described to me what taking Ketamine feels like: you're standing in a long corridor lined with doors. Each door leads somewhere but as you stand, the doors slam shut, hard, one after another. All that's left is you, in a great long echoing hallway that goes nowhere with locked doors going on forever.

I can't think. Every word I carve out of the rock with my fingernails, groping all the time for meaning in the darkness, the shape of things familiar and yet unknown. I'm aware of the things I know, but locked away somewhere, and I don't have the password to open the doors again.

There are tears under the surface somewhere, bitter tears full of self-pity and reproach. None of your sweet tears of release. These are pure acid and I will not shed them. They'll corrode everything they touch.

So I sit, silent and unable to reach out and watch like a prisoner in a tower, waiting in that endless corridor, in the fading hope that one of those doors might not be locked after all.

It's as close to dying as you can get, I think.

For people who have no experience personally of depression, I'd like to remind them that it is an illness, it's not something a person suffering with it

71

chooses to endure. Nobody enjoys it and it's as damaging and debilitating as an illness or injury that can be seen plainly. I don't write these sorts of things as a bid for attention, but initially as a way of trying to understand what happens to me, and I share some of them as a part of widening awareness of an issue that is still somehow taboo. People who know me in the so-called 'real world' are shocked to discover I have this illness because most of the time I hide it. When I suffer with the onset, I find I stop being able to talk. I can still write, usually, but my normal loquacious self vanishes and I will fall silent. I can still come out with the one-liners and the quick comebacks but only as a default setting. I don't find them funny myself; it's just a way of diverting attention.

An 'Unsound Mind' – bringing a family history into the open.

Suzie Grogan

I have, over the past two or three years, been unlocking metaphorical cupboards to find metaphorical skeletons falling at me from all sides. Inspired less by 'Who Do You Think You Are' than by an indecent fascination with the minutiae of other people's lives ('nosiness' I believe is an alternative word, an inability to mind my own business) I have been looking into my family history. Not all of it you understand. More thorough members of my family have done a terrific job of listing the details of most key branches, and have found that on the whole my background is dull and singularly uninteresting, on paper at least. However, there has always been some mystery over my maternal line. My mother has recreated for me a shadowy late-Victorian, Edwardian and post Great War North London past, populated with stories of aunts reputed to be Vera Drake-like back street abortionists, shiftless uncles, haunted houses and a silver-smithing grandfather who engraved the trowel that laid the first brick of the Albert Hall. With a fascination for Victorian London already well established, how could I resist the opportunity to delve a little further? What I found in fact, was a story 10 times more interesting than anticipated, with a vein of deep sadness running through it, and not a little sheer horror. Digging into my family history has in fact uncovered years of unrecognised, or hidden, struggles with mental health issues. A denial that left my closest relations vulnerable and resulted in at least two fatalities.

The cutting illustrating this piece relates to my Great Uncle Alfred Hardiman, who at the end of 1922 murdered his ex-girlfriend, Ellen Street, with a cut-throat razor and then turned the weapon on himself and committed suicide by slitting his own throat. Horrific. The amount of blood is unimaginable. What was somehow as shocking though was that Bessie Hardiman, identified in the cutting as present at the time of the deaths, gave evidence at the inquest. She is my Grandma. She had never mentioned this incident to my mother, even when as an adult she would surely have been more understanding than shocked. I found the cutting purely by chance, in an online newspaper archive. It uncovered a mystery that explained many whispered conversations she had half heard, half understood as a child. 'Poor Alf,' her family would say, 'it was the war you know.' I checked his WW1 records, expecting to find years in the trenches of the Somme. Instead I saw that he had spent less than a year in the army in 1917, based in Mill Hill, North London. I can't find much detail, but he was discharged as unfit, owing to 'enuresis'. The poor man was incontinent. Whatever had affected my great uncle, it was not the trauma of the front line. Whatever it was and I suspect it was his mental state, almost certainly went untreated.

When faced with this story, one that I was afraid to discuss with her for a while, my mother was surprised of course, but not astonished, as I thought she would be. Recalling her childhood in the same house, the same kitchen (a small thing worries me still – who mopped up all the blood? My Grandma?) in which the murder and suicide occurred, it was clear that her other uncle, Alf's brother, was also fragile in some ill-defined way, finding steady employment difficult. A sister too suffered with depression later in life, and one ended her days in a north London mental hospital. But the family had moved from overcrowded Victorian Clerkenwell out to the newly built suburbs of Hornsey and Holloway and mental health issues were something of a taboo as they painstakingly worked their way up a perceived social ladder. It was a time of judgmental curtain twitching, when society's view was very 'stiff upper lip' and 'pull yourself together', or risk being locked away in any number of institutions that I still remember from my childhood – Colney Hatch, Shenley – and much suffering and injustice must have been caused by this widespread attitude.

I looked back further, at census returns from 1881. Alf's mother was there described in classic late Victorian terms as a 'lunatic'. His father, my mother's silversmith grandfather, had children both with his wife and with the family servant alternately in the same decade. It was clearly not a straightforward upbringing.

This was all news to my mum, and it set us thinking, and talking, about how this might in some way explain the breakdown my uncle, mum's brother, had in his forties when he achieved a promotion he simply couldn't cope with. I remember, as a teenager, the much-loved man that my siblings and I treated almost as an older brother, turning up on our doorstep. He had got on his train as usual, but something had snapped and he found himself simply unable to get to work. I can picture myself as a child standing at the kitchen window, watching as he stood in our garden in tears talking to my mum. How accurate this recollection is I can't say, but my mother's explanation that his lifelong anxiety had all stemmed from their being evacuated at the start of WWII may have been a little simplistic. With her care he recovered, but was never really well again.

I am like my uncle in some ways. I am able and well-qualified. I perform well at interviews. But somehow, whatever it is that drives others onwards to levels of stress on which they thrive, for my uncle and I it would drive us downwards, into episodes of depression and anxiety that meant, and means for me, that life can be difficult to deal with. My uncle died of a heart attack, aged just 49.

I can't say that I have inherited a gene, or developed depression and anxiety through any family trait that stems from a one-sided family history. Others could better describe the likelihood of a genetic link, or what life was like for those with mental illness of any kind in the first half of the 20th century. I had a loving and supportive upbringing, with parents who doted on me and my sister and brother. But for some reason I have developed a mental illness that, with the support of my GP, my family and a little medication, I am at last finding a way to cope with. My poor mum still feels it must have been something she did or failed to do when I was a child that has caused my distress, and I cannot dissuade her from those thoughts. This is why, for me, it is desperately important to raise awareness of mental health issues. Honesty and openness are vital if we are to end stigma and discrimination. I am fortunate that I live in more enlightened times than Alfred Hardiman, whose crime of passion was terrible, but whose 'unsound mind' was probably one desperately in need of the help that should be available to anyone experiencing the effects of mental distress.

Bibliography, links & suggestions for further reading

Suggested reading

Books by contributors or mentioned in the text

Underneath the Lemon Tree, Mark Rice-Oxley (Little, Brown 2012)

Dodging Suicide, Kit Johnson (CreateSpace 2011)

The Thing Inside My Head: A Family's Journey through Mental Illness, Lois Chaber (Chipmunka 2008)

The Confidence Gap by Russ Ballard

Writing Therapy, Tim Atkinson (Dotterel Press 2010)

Other recommended titles

Sunbathing in the Rain: A Cheerful Book About Depression, Gwyneth Lewis (Harper Perennial 2006)

Shoot the Damn Dog – A Memoir of Depression, Sally Brampton (Bloomsbury, 2008)

Counselling for Toads: A Psychological Adventure, Robert de Board (Routledge 1997)

Websites

Mind	www.mind.org.uk
Sane	www.sane.org.uk
Time to Change	www.time-to-change.org.uk
Samaritans	www.samaritans.org
Rethink	www.rethink.org
Black Dog Tribe	www.blackdogtribe.com
Mental Health Foundation	www.mentalhealth.org.uk
Young Minds	www.youngminds.org.uk

Acknowledgements

Although it is exciting to have one's work in print, everyone who contributed to the production of this book did so in order to raise funds for mental health charities and to raise awareness of mental health issues. Despite recent publicity there is still a stigma attached to being open about depression and anxiety. So 'thank you' to everyone who has given so freely of their time to support me.

I am very grateful to Tim Atkinson and Gareth Dearson at Dotterel Press for having faith in this project and thank them for their confidence. Thanks to Rin Simpson for her invaluable help with editing the manuscript. I was far too close to it at times to be truly objective about the contents. Rin is also responsible for putting me in touch with the remarkable Ingrid Smejkal of Ingrid Eva Creative who produced an original artwork for the cover of this book, waiving her fee and being incredibly helpful with her suggestions. Similarly, Nettie Edwards is responsible for the beautiful artwork within the pages, offering me the use of her photographs and adapting them for the needs of the book. Thank you to them both.

Of course this book wouldn't be possible without all those willing to share their stories for my blog and then for this book. Mental illness is an illness like any other but voicing the experience still leaves people open to prejudice in a way that is different. I cannot thank you all enough for having such strength and courage.

This book has taken over my life for a while now but I have thoroughly enjoyed the process. None of it would have been possible without the support of my husband Peter who has given me more than he knows over the years.

And thank you to everyone who has bought this book. The only way the project could be a success is because you have handed over your money and supported it. The charities who will receive every penny of profit made from the sales will make good use of the funds raised.

Finally, I hope you find this book as rewarding to read as it was to put together.

Dandelions & Bad Hair Days…

Artwork on cover by Ingrid Eva Creative
Photographs by Nettie Edwards